FRIENDS OF THE EARTH
HANDBOOK

FRIENDS OF THE EARTH HANDBOOK

EDITED BY
JONATHON PORRITT

ILLUSTRATED BY CHRIS WINN

An OPTIMA book

© Friends of the Earth 1987

First published in 1987 by
Macdonald Optima, a division of
Macdonald & Co. (Publishers) Ltd
Reprinted 1987
Reprinted 1988

A Member of Maxwell Pergamon Publishing Corporation Plc

BRITISH LIBRARY CATALOGUING IN PUBLICATION DATA

Friends of the Earth handbook.
  1. Conservation of natural resources——
Amateurs' manuals
I. Porritt, Jonathon
333.7'2   S938

  ISBN 0-356-12560-2

Macdonald & Co. (Publishers) Ltd
3rd Floor
Greater London House
Hampstead Road
London NW1 7QX

Photoset in 11 point Century Schoolbook by
  Ａ Tek Art Limited, Croydon, Surrey

Printed and bound in Great Britain by
The Guernsey Press Co. Ltd,
Guernsey, Channel Islands

ACKNOWLEDGMENT

Friends of the Earth would like to thank all those who have contributed to this book, with particular thanks to Angela Henderson and Peter Draper.

CONTENTS

INTRODUCTION

The *Friends of the Earth Handbook* is for people interested in looking after their environment, and who want answers to the question, how? How to save energy, how to eat wisely, how to protect our environment, how to look after our health, how to act as responsible consumers – in short, how to tread more lightly on this planet of ours. We may know what we should be doing, but not always how best to be doing it. Our *Handbook*, written by staff and supporters of Friends of the Earth, sets the issues in context and provides the kind of practical advice we all need to become good environmentalists, with a useful resources section at the end of each chapter.

Friends of the Earth is one of the leading environmental pressure organizations in Britain, and a major force behind today's growing Green Movement.

Our message is a simple one: it is only by protecting the Earth that we can protect ourselves – against pollution, the destruction of our urban and rural environment, mass unemployment and the horrors of global famine and war.

This is a message which – at last – is beginning to be taken seriously by politicians and economists. Their concern is genuine. But their readiness to act is still very limited.

And that's where Friends of the Earth comes in. It is our role to put the pressure on politicians and decision-makers at every level. Changes in the law and public opinion are testimony to our successes.

Such pressure is vital if we are ever to learn to live in harmony with the Earth, and thus to improve standards of living and the real quality of lives everywhere.

JONATHON PORRITT
Director, Friends of the Earth

1.
YOU AND YOUR ENVIRONMENT

Suddenly 'the environment' is popping up everywhere. Previously relegated to the second or third division of political issues, it's now up there among the leaders. Where once the media spurned environmental stories, they now seek them out, high and low. And though it may once have been considered eccentric to get uptight about pollution or saving the whale, today it's the environment-bashers who are seen as the weirdos. Everyone (well, almost everyone) would seem to be going green.

Fine. Better late than never. But when it actually comes down to knowing what to do, it's more easily theorized about than put into practice. The question now isn't 'why', but 'how'. If the planet really is up the spout, what can you or I do about it?

That, in a 100% organic pesticide-free nutshell, is what this book is all about. If you seek the all-too-familiar catalogues of doom, rhetoric about the destructiveness of human beings, or a scientific treatise, then you must look elsewhere (turn to page 26 to see exactly where to look). *This* book is about you, your environment, and what you can do in specific and practical terms. Ditch the despair, put aside the cynicism, hive off the hopelessness; the world is there for the saving, and it's up to you.

WHO, ME?

Hopelessness and helplessness are predictable responses to the current state of affairs. What can one individual do to alleviate the symptoms of the massive environmental decline of the last 40 years? Just how many signatures have to be raised for a petition, how many organizations joined and protest letters written, how much jumble sold and leaflets delivered, to achieve *any* significant advance in the campaign against today's planet-wasters?

I'm afraid the answer is still 'a lot' – millions, many, hundreds, tons, and thousands. Our environment (and that means *us*) is still on the receiving end of a fearsome barrage of attacks. In this book we concentrate on the problems of energy and transport, countryside and land use, food and health, wastefulness and pollution – but this list is by no means comprehensive.

To balance that, as we will see in Chapter Two, there is much good news to celebrate. The Green Movement is on the up and up, and the politicians know it. The prospect of real change is in the air.

Too little and too late, do I hear you say? And what about the rest of the world? How can we not despair when confronted with megaproblems like the continuing famine in the Third World, the inexorable spread of the deserts, the loss of the world's rainforests, massive erosion of grasslands and croplands, the economic damage caused by a lunatic spiral of arms spending, rising populations, acid rain, and the build-up of carbon dioxide in the atmosphere? But recognition of the scale of the problem calls for an ever more urgent response. As the *Global 2000 Report* to the US President put it in 1982, 'given the urgency, scope, and complexity of the challenges before us, the efforts now underway around the world fall far short of what is needed. An era of unprecedented global cooperation and commitment is essential.'

It shouldn't come as a surprise that our own welfare is intimately related to the welfare of all the other people in the world; indeed, to that of all living things. But for many people it still does. It still isn't commonly understood that what people do and the way they behave materially affect biological systems on the other side of the planet. One of the greatest challenges we face is to drive home this inescapable ecological truth: we are all connected and we are all interdependent.

You can't get more global than that. But as we all know, nothing is likely to happen globally before it happens locally. Which brings us to personal responsibility.

RESPONSIBILITY: THE FIRST LINK

When you drink too much, you get a hangover. The connection is direct and pretty immediate. The responsibility is yours and yours alone.

When you choose to buy ordinary eggs, you may be a few pence better off for not having bought free-range eggs, but as a direct consequence quite needless suffering is inflicted on the hens which produced those eggs. The responsibility is *partly* yours; you are just one among the many involved in the suffering of battery chickens.

When you can't be bothered to insulate your loft, or even turn off a few lights, energy is wasted, more electricity has to be generated, and more fossil fuels have to be burnt. As a result, the long-term safety of millions of people living at or near sea level will be threatened because of the build-up of carbon dioxide in the atmosphere. Your responsibility for this may be pretty remote, since almost everyone is involved, but it is still there.

Our lives are invisibly wrapped around with 'chains of responsibility'. Some are very short, with just one or two links between what we do and the consequences of what we do. Some are quite long, with many links in the chain, though we can still see where it all ends. Some are so long that it is much easier not to work out where all the links are leading; the burden of responsibility can sometimes get a little too weighty.

But the readiness of people to change their ways is in direct proportion to their willingness to examine the links in the chain. Bob Geldof broke all the 'rules' of charitable fundraising by down-playing the conventional themes of pity ('look at that starving child; isn't it tragic') and guilt ('look at that starving child; just think how rich we are in comparison') and emphasizing instead responsibility ('look at that starving child; starving because of the way *we* live'). For millions of people, the chain suddenly shortened. The famine wasn't an 'act of God', or 'their own fault', or 'an inevitable tragedy'. The suffering in Africa was linked to our own living standards, our political systems, our values. And so it became that much easier, and that much more compelling, to do something about it.

Once the links in any chain of responsibility are understood, we can decide what to do about it. With the famine in Africa, most people dug into their pockets and gave what they could. Others took part in or organized fundraising events. There was a huge upsurge in the number of people volunteering for work in the developing countries.

Some took action nearer to home. Making a direct connection between the death of 40,000 children every day in the Third World, and the UK grain mountain of 4 million tonnes (built up at a direct cost of £900 million to the British taxpayer, plus an annual bill of around £180 million just for storage), they protested outside the warehouses where this wasted grain is quietly rotting away, rapidly becoming unfit for human consumption.

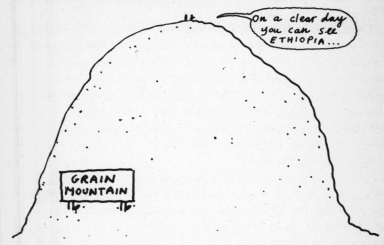

A few people symbolically removed some bags of grain 'to put it to better use', and now face serious charges of burglary – for doing what most of us would surely believe to be the right thing.

FROM THEORY TO PRACTICE

You can see this variety of response in many environmental campaigns. Chapter Three looks in some detail at the success of the 'Save the Whale Campaign', and shows how the actions of millions of individuals, from simple signatures on a petition, to parliamentary lobbying, to the extraordinary courage of the Greenpeace protesters, *collectively* managed to reduce commercial whaling to the level that it has reached today.

It often doesn't matter what we do as long as we do something. It may well start with something very small, seemingly very insignificant in comparison to the scale of the problem. After all, are we all really going to save the world's rainforests by not buying a mahogany loo-seat? Answers in Chapter Three, but let's assume for the time being that it will at least help!

Nor do we have to think of giving up the world in order to save it. It won't be necessary for anybody reading this book to become a nut-eating hermit, renouncing all worldly pleasures in a self-satisfied convulsion of green puritanism. In giving up some things, we take up others – often better, more satisfying, more enjoyable. In doing more with less, the cup of life still runneth over.

Nor do we all have to leap into little rubber boats and fling ourselves before the juggernaut of industrial progress. Death-defying feats of eco-heroism are fine, but not for all of us. In fact, saving the world is often a pretty humdrum, lowly affair.

But two things *must* happen: at a certain point, awareness of our individual responsibility must result in real change. There are just so many times you can assuage a vaguely troubled conscience with promises of *mañana, mañana*, before it becomes straightforward hypocrisy. First and foremost, it is the escalation of individual consumption (as much as, if not more than, the increase in absolute human numbers) that has had such an adverse impact on the quality of our environment.

And secondly, individual responsibility must be set within the context of collective action. If it is indeed true that no man – or woman – is an island unto themselves, then bridge-building and collective action become essential components of anybody's personal commitment. Solitary greenery can be pretty soul-destroying.

Individually accepting responsibility for the way we live, and collectively taking action to do something about it, allows us to restore a sense of balance between ourselves and the economic order within which we operate. Moreover, it helps us to improve the material and spiritual quality of our lives – and that's exactly what the rest of this book is about.

2.
GREENS ARE GOOD FOR YOU!

Students of language development and political change
will one day have a fine time tracing the explosive growth
of all things 'green' during the 1980s. Though it remains
frustratingly hard to pin down, many commentators
accept that the arrival of green politics will be seen as
one of the most significant features of a decade when
many people and politicians seemed to have lost their
way.

Characteristically, it's not even possible to give one
simple definition of the word 'green' – it's used in many
different contexts by many different people. For most
people, however, 'green' means 'environmental', so
today's Green Movement is seen as an extension of the

Environment Movement of the '70s and the Conservation Movement of the '60s. As we shall see, to limit the meaning of green to matters environmental would nonetheless be misleading – and ultimately detrimental to the future of green politics.

The Green Movement has been described by the Italian scientist Aurelio Peccei as 'a kind of popular army, with a function comparable to that of the antibodies generated to restore normal conditions in a diseased biological organism', and in a rather different vein by Jonathon Porritt, the author of *Seeing Green*, as 'a vast and diverse profusion of plant life materializing on the top of an abandoned dung heap, weeds, flowers, creepers, brambles, herbs – each different, yet each a part of an intricate interdependent pattern of fertility and green growth'.

Some commentators are not so complimentary, preferring to rely on the tired old insults and put-downs of the '70s, if only to protect themselves against the terrifying realization that their tired old world is falling to pieces around them.

BACKGROUND GREEN

But it is important to remember that we are still talking about a very young movement. In the latter half of the '70s, environment and peace groups in the UK and elsewhere were going through a difficult time. The anti-nuclear movement was spurred by the vitality and determination of their colleagues in France and Germany; conservationists waxed indignant against the destruction of the countryside by modern farming, but nothing much happened as a result. Indeed, green issues barely surfaced in the British 1979 General Election.

But behind the scenes, things were really beginning to move, particularly in Europe. In 1979, a co-ordination group of all the European green parties was set up, and in 1981 the Belgian green parties (Ecolo, the French-speaking party, and Agalev, their Flemish counterparts) achieved the first significant electoral breakthrough when five Senators and four MPs were elected.

The German Green Party formally came into being in January 1980, after several years of uncertainty within the anti-nuclear and environment movements about the desirability of establishing a *separate* party. The German Greens rapidly made their mark: under an electoral system which determines representation *proportionately*, once a 5% threshold has been crossed, they first won seats in the regional parliaments and then really caught the headlines with the election of 28 MPs to the Bundestag in 1983.

Since then they've rarely been out of the news. Their penchant for self-destructive clumsiness has aggravated even their warmest supporters, but their fiercely radical stance on many issues has provided some real opposition within the German system. And their influence has been considerable; the environment is now far better defended and the cause of peace far better promoted than they were before their dramatic arrival on the scene.

Meanwhile, the Ecology Party in Britain, dealing with a very different electoral system, looked enviously at what was happening in Germany. But politicians of other colours, never slow to grasp potential political advantage, were beginning to take notice too. The word 'green' began to infiltrate itself into all sorts of hitherto alien territory; the major parties learned how to wrap their tongues around it, and *Hansard*, the daily reports of Parliamentary proceedings, had difficulty deciding between 'green' or just plain green, a nice reflection of the growing respectability of a new idea.

At the same time, the media began to get the hang of it. Cottoning on to the fact that three million people in the UK were members of one green organization or another, the number of stories and programmes gradually began to increase. By the mid 1980s, green issues were firmly on the map, and in recent months there has been an unprecedented explosion of greenery, with editorials, major features, and extensive TV coverage.

The cynics remain unmoved: just a green flash in the pan, they say, a fashionable spasm similar to that at the end of the '60s during the hippy era. The cynics are always worth listening to, but in this case they are almost certainly wrong, for the change this time is much more profound and much more far-reaching than ever before.

This analysis is strongly reinforced by what is happening elsewhere. In many other parts of the world, there has been a surge of green activity: in Australia, where a unique 'Green Ban' movement brought together trade unionists, activists and local residents to oppose a whole series of destructive developments; in New Zealand, whose determined efforts to remain 'nuclear-free', refusing entry to all US warships that might be carrying nuclear weapons, has won international acclaim; throughout the Pacific, where many of the islands have become increasingly active in rejecting their enforced involvement in the nuclear arms race; in India, where the implications of the environmental devastation of the last twenty years have at last been recognized by top politicians, including Rajiv Gandhi; in the Far East and South America, which are now beginning to see the emergence of powerful environmental groups despite considerable political difficulties in many countries; and even in Eastern Europe, networks and organizations, both official and unofficial, are at last coming together − especially in the wake of Chernobyl.

And greens are really on the boil in the United States! Much of the written work that has underpinned the development of worldwide green politics and philosophy has been done in the States, and there is in general a higher awareness about green issues than in Europe. Moreover, the green threads are now beginning to emerge from a veritable patchwork quilt of progressive organizations, to be found in the women's movement, the civil rights movement, the bioregionalist movement, the peace and anti-nuclear movements and all those involved in 'voluntary simplicity' or lifestyle changes. As yet, no coherent strategy for the development of green politics has emerged; it is as if all the many different patches of the quilt are still lying around on the floor waiting to be stitched together! Given both the scale and the teeming diversity of the United States, this is hardly surprising, and the vitality of the environment movement remains undiminished by a lack of central co-ordination.

THE UK GREENS

On a smaller scale, exactly the same kind of diversity and vitality characterizes the Green Movement in the UK. It is not easy identifying all the constituent parts of such a movement. Far and away the most useful and comprehensive reference book in this context is Michael Barker's *Directory for the Environment*, which gives details of over 1,400 organizations involved in one way or another on the UK environment scene.

The best way of making sense of this profusion of organizations is to consider them in terms of their function. By far the largest category in this respect is that of the pressure group – whose job it is to pressure elected representatives, ministers, central government and local administrators, by monitoring the actions of these decision-makers and by assiduously lobbying them to change their ways, by undertaking appropriate research and by submitting evidence, by putting forward constructive proposals as well as by putting the boot in where necessary, and by organizing demonstrations or taking direct action where appropriate.

Some organizations are multi-issue pressure groups (like Friends of the Earth, which runs at least ten different campaigns, and Greenpeace); some are single-issue pressure groups, but with a very broad range of interests (like the World Wildlife Fund and the Council for the Protection of Rural England); and some stick to just one specific issue (like the Royal Society for the Protection of Birds, the Campaign for Lead-Free Air and many of the animal welfare and animal rights groups).

All these pressure groups are strictly non-party political: their function is to influence politicians and voters of *all* persuasions. A rather different function is carried out by those groups operating within political parties, such as the Socialist Environment and Resources Association and the Socialist Countryside Group within the Labour Party, or the Liberal Ecology Group and the SDP Greens within the Alliance. (I'm sorry to say that not a lot has been heard recently of the Conservative Ecology Group!)

The Green Party, formerly the Ecology Party, stands deliberately outside the system and challenges the major parties by confronting them directly. Without proportional representation in Britain, it is an uphill battle to get Green candidates elected, but there is no doubt that the Green Party has played a significant role over the last few years in the gradual greening that has gone on within the other parties. It has also spawned organizations like Green CND, now an increasingly influential voice within the Campaign for Nuclear Disarmament, and The Other Economic Summit, which is far and away the most effective organization dealing with alternative economics.

Then there's a whole range of groups that have more to do with changes in lifestyle (such as the Vegetarian Society or the Lifestyle Movement), with practical action (such as the British Trust for Conservation Volunteers or the Groundwork Trusts), with education (such as the Council for Environmental Education or the Centre for Alternative Technology), or with academic research (such as the Political Ecology Research Group and Earth Resources Research). And finally, there are many people who choose to get involved in *local* environmental organizations or amenity groups rather than nationally, and a whole heap more who don't happen to belong to any organization, but whose lifestyle or work is decidedly green.

THE MAJOR PARTIES

It's hardly surprising that such a ferment of activity has had a profound effect on *all* the political parties. The SDP made an impressive start with the publication of *Conservation and Change* in 1985: lots of fudging on difficult issues, but clear and concise in its overall perception of just how serious things had become. Perhaps a little piqued by the SDP's commendable opportunism, the Liberal Party (always the front-runner among the major parties) spent the next year getting its environment policy in order, producing a sequence of internal discussion documents which have become gradually better. But a powerful and somewhat reactionary farming lobby within the Liberal Party has meant that their countryside policies are inadequate, hesitant and defensive; they might have worked in the '70s, but are now something of an embarrassment.

The Labour Party was quick to seize on this, and in August 1986 produced an excellent document on the environment. The result of lengthy consultation with environmental groups, this draft policy should have guaranteed the Labour Party maximum credibility. Unfortunately, in the hands of their fanatically pronuclear environment spokesman, Dr Jack Cunningham, its impact was not as far reaching as it should have been. It was like composing a violin concerto and handing it over for performance to a tone-deaf banjo-player.

For reasons known only to themselves, Conservative leaders have decided they are going to have no truck with all this green nonsense, but just carry on as before. This means that even the things they *do* do (such as the creation of a unified Pollution Inspectorate or the introduction of Environmentally Sensitive Areas) are done belatedly, grudgingly and without adequate funding. A growing green element within the Conservative Party, conspicuously and astutely led by William Waldegrave, is getting more and more frustrated – and with good cause, for conservation and Conservatism could so easily go hand in hand instead of being seen as mutually exclusive.

The cynics are, of course, right to point out that in all the parties there's a strong element of unapologetic vote-grabbing behind all this greenery. After all, the green vote could well decide the outcome of several marginal constituencies at the next general election. It's also true that, while all this is going on, the state of the environment goes on deteriorating, as will be made very clear throughout the remaining chapters. But for all that, it must be recognized that such unprecedented ferment signifies *genuine* political change, the true significance of which will only become apparent over the next few years.

GREEN PRINCIPLES

It's often convenient for its opponents to see the Green Movement as a ramshackle coalition. But don't be fooled by the apparent incoherence; there is enough common ground to establish the foundations for a real breakthrough in green politics, common ground that is based on certain fundamental principles:

- a reverence for the earth and all its creatures;
- protection of the environment as a precondition of a prosperous, healthy society;
- sustainable alternatives to the rat race of economic growth;
- a recognition of the rights of future generations in our use of all resources;
- open, participatory democracy at every level of society.

The principles are easily stated. The means by which they are achieved remain a little more elusive. It is hardly surprising that there should be intense controversy about these means, and that the different organizations should therefore operate in very different ways. One of these controversies is to do with the fundamental nature of our environmental predicament; on one side are the 'reformers', on the other the 'radicals'.

The reformers would argue that we can improve the existing system bit by bit until it both meets our needs *and* conforms to green principles. The radicals would dispute this, claiming that the whole industrial system is inherently corrupt and unsustainable, and that only a rapid shift to a very different economic and social system will do the job.

This clash between the 'light greens' and the 'dark greens' will become increasingly important over the next few years. We are on the threshold of significant reforms in environmental and resource management. Years of persistent, unrelenting pressure are about to pay off, and the dedication of thousands of environmentalists will be rewarded. But the question now is, just *how* significant are these reforms? Have we perhaps taken two steps back while stumbling one step forward? And if we lift our eyes from our own narrow horizons, aren't the prospects for the developing world so gloomy as to set at nought the achievement of our own thin green line?

Throughout its history, the Green Movement has been known for its chronic gloom-and-doom-mongering. Dire warnings have been uttered at every conceivable opportunity; some have turned out to be correct, others not. But as we move towards the end of the '80s, restrained optimism rather than fatalistic pessimism would seem to be the order of the day. Such optimism derives mainly from the large numbers of people in this country actively engaged in finding ways of living more ecologically, and in accepting their responsibility for what happens both near to home and in the rest of the world.

RESOURCES

Books:

Michael Barker (ed.), *The Directory for the Environment* (Routledge & Kegan Paul, 1986)

Lester Brown, *Building a Sustainable Society* (W W Norton, New York, 1981)

Fritjof Capra, *The Turning Point* (Wildwood House, 1982)

Erik Eckholm, *Down to Earth* (Pluto Press, 1982)

Ronald Higgins, *The Seventh Enemy* (Hodder & Stoughton, 1978)

John McCormick, *The User's Guide to the Environment* (Kogan Page, 1983)

Aurelio Peccei, *100 Pages for the Future* (Futura, 1982)

Jonathon Porritt, *Seeing Green* (Blackwell, 1984)

Theodore Roszak, *Person/Planet* (Granada, 1981)

Fritz Schumacher, *Small is Beautiful* (Abacus, 1974)

Charlene Spretnak and Fritjof Capra, *Green Politics* (Hutchinson, 1984)

Des Wilson (editor), *The Environmental Crisis* (Heinemann, 1984)

Magazines:
The Ecologist,
  Worthyvale Manor, Camelford, Cornwall
Green Line,
  34 Cowley Rd, Oxford OX4 1HZ
New Internationalist,
  42 Hythe Bridge Street, Oxford OX1 2EP
Resurgence,
  Ford House, Hartland, Bideford, Devon

Contacts and organizations:
These are just a *few* contact points. If you want to know,
get yourself a copy of *The Directory for the Environment*
referred to opposite.

GENERAL
Council for the Protection of Rural England,
  4 Hobart Place, London SW1W 0HY
Friends of the Earth,
  377 City Rd, London EC1V 1NA
Green Alliance,
  60 Chandos Place, London WC2N 4HG
Greenpeace,
  36 Graham Street, London N1
World Wildlife Fund,
  Panda House, 11-13 Ockford Rd, Godalming, Surrey
  GU7 1QU

CONSERVATION
British Trust for Conservation Volunteers,
  36 St Mary's Street, Wallingford, Oxon OX10 0EU
Royal Society for Nature Conservation,
  The Green, Nettleham, Lincoln LN2 2NR
Royal Society for the Protection of Birds,
  The Lodge, Sandy, Beds SG19 2DL

POLITICAL
Conservative Ecology Group,
  51 Stakes Hill Rd, Waterlooville, Hants PO7 7LD

Green Party,
  36-38 Clapham Rd, London SW9 0JQ
Liberal Ecology Group,
  77 Dresden Rd, London N19 3BG
SDP Greens,
  69 Cambridge Rd, Oakington, Cambridge, CB4 5BG
Socialist Environment & Resources Association,
  9 Poland Street, London W1

ANIMALS
Animal Aid,
  7 Castle Street, Tonbridge, Kent TN9 1BH
British Union for the Abolition of Vivisection,
  16A Crane Grove, Islington, London N7 8LB
Compassion in World Farming,
  20 Lavant Street, Petersfield, Hants GU32 3EW

PEACE
Campaign Against the Arms Trade,
  11 Goodwin Street, London, N4 3HQ
Campaign for Nuclear Disarmament,
  22-24 Underwood Street, London N1 7JQ
Green CND,
  23 Lower Street, Stroud, Glos GL5 2HT

EDUCATION AND RESEARCH
Council for Environmental Education,
  School of Education, University of Reading,
  London Rd, Reading, Berks RG1 5AQ
Conservation Trust,
  George Palmer School, Northumberland Ave, Reading,
  Berks RG2 0EN
Political Ecology Research Group,
  34 Cowley Rd, Oxford OX4 1H2

ECONOMICS AND TECHNOLOGY
Centre for Alternative Technology,
  Llwyngwern Quarry, Machynlleth, Powys
  SY20 9A2

Intermediate Technology & Development Group,
  Myson House, Railway Terrace, Rugby, Warwicks
  CU21 3HT
The Other Economic Summit,
  42 Warriner Gardens, London SW11 4DU

SPECIAL INTERESTS
CLEAR (Campaign for Lead-Free Air),
  2 Northdown Street, London N1 9BG
Civic Trust,
  17 Carlton House Terrace, London SW1Y 5AW
Groundwork Foundation,
  27 Mawdsley Street, Bolton, Lancs B4 1LN
Lifestyle Movement,
  Manor Farm, Little Gidding, Huntingdon, Cambs PE17
  5RJ
Population Concern,
  231 Tottenham Court Rd, London W1P 0HY
Soil Association,
  86 Colston Street, Bristol BS1 5BB
Town & Country Planning Association,
  17 Carlton House Terrace, London SW1Y 5AS
TRANSPORT 2000,
  Walkden House, 10 Melton Street, London NW1 2EJ

3.
CONSUMER POWER

Anti-apartheid campaigners go into a supermarket and pile a trolley high with goods labelled 'Produce of South Africa'. After the total has been rung up, they refuse to pay on principle, emphasizing how international trade bolsters unacceptable political repression, and walk out, leaving behind the bemused cashier and a supermarket manager with a headache – it takes a long time to replace all those items and clear the till.

If you're stuck in the queue behind such determined campaigners, it may take a little while to appreciate the moral of the story. But actions like this carried out on a nationwide basis can provoke a lot of people to think about how they inadvertently help perpetuate economic or political relationships they would probably condemn once they recognized them. Moreover, it makes the managements of supermarket chains reconsider their buying strategies, if only to placate angry customers.

The steady trend away from South African goods makes one thing clear: individuals *can* make a difference. Given a little bit of time, energy, knowledge and commitment, individuals can make a *big* difference. In recent years there have been many instances where small groups of people working together have played a crucial role in ensuring the success of international campaigns. The campaigns to stop the trade in endangered species and to save the whales are two famous examples. In each case, simple actions by individuals led to political change and the success of the campaign.

SAVE THE WHALE!

For decades, the whaling industry typified the ignorant and shortsighted approach to resources. In their attempts to get rich as fast as possible, the whalers sent species after species to the edge of extinction. The magnificent blue whale, the largest creature on earth, with veins big enough for a child to crawl through, and the slow-moving hump-back were the first to become commercially extinct. Unperturbed, the whalers simply switched to other species – the fin, sei, sperm and eventually the minke, the smallest commercially hunted baleen whale.

Concerted international lobbying by conservation organizations, such as direct action to confront whaling ships about their bloody business, rallies attended by thousands, letter-writing campaigns to politicians, and local media coverage of the plight of these irreplaceable creatures, slowly brought results. To start with, the International Whaling Commission gradually lowered quotas, and one by one most nations gave up whaling in favour of protectionist policies. But a hard core of committed nations, notably Japan, Norway, Russia and Iceland, annually lodged official objections to reduced quotas or proposed bans, as they were legally entitled to do under the International Whaling Convention. And markets for whale products persisted (oils for leather industries and the military, soaps and candles, meat for petfood, ambergris for perfumes) even in countries like Britain, which were officially against commercial whaling.

In the late 1970s, conservationists took the campaign to the high streets of Britain. The precedent was already there. In 1972, a campaign organized by Friends of the Earth to persuade consumers not to buy fur coats made from tiger, leopard and cheetah skins had been entirely successful, leading to a ban on the sale of these 'goods'. This time the goal was more ambitious: an international ban on the sale or manufacture of all items containing whale by-products.

Friends of the Earth produced lists of goods containing whale products and their manufacturers, and circulated these lists to local activists. Local groups picketed shops and leafleted consumers, pointing out the alternatives. Demand for these products fell and concern from retailers – in many cases sympathetic to the conservation cause – led to producers withdrawing products. By 1st January 1982, when an EEC Directive banned the trade in whale products in Europe, most were already off the market.

Similarly, in the USA, Greenpeace recently co-ordinated a boycott of Norwegian fish as part of their continuing anti-whaling campaign. Large businesses, aware of the power of the conservationists in the marketplace, cancelled more than ten million dollars' worth of Norwegian fish contracts.

In 1985, Norway exported $350M of fish to the USA. Her whaling industry is worth less than $2M. Confronted with such stark economic reality, even the threat of an embargo or a consumer boycott cannot be lightly shrugged off.

In Britain, the International Federation for Animal Welfare's campaign against the notorious Canadian harp seal hunt led Tesco to stop buying Canadian fish products until the hunt stops, and led the EEC to ban the sale of goods using the fur of baby harp seals.

Industrial growth-oriented economies are dominated by large commercial organizations keen to maximize production. Short-term profit motives drive market forces. Individuals in capitalist democracies are not encouraged to participate in decision-making, but merely to sit back and enjoy a never-ending flow of material goods. It's easy to feel lost in such a system. As Duane Elgin, author of *Voluntary Simplicity*, acidly noted, advertising, particularly on television, creates 'an electronic dictatorship that promotes extravagant consumption, social passivity and personal impotence.'

In the race for growth, corporations and governments often ignore the effects of their expanding production. Non-renewable resources such as minerals are still treated as inexhaustible supplies that will always be available, despite clear warnings to the contrary. Even potentially renewable ones such as tropical hardwoods are 'mined' rather than harvested, with little thought for the future. Indeed, scarcity if anything drives the price up, leading to increased profitability, but often at the expense of our long-term social and environmental well-being. To many of us it is obvious that such shortsighted operations are ultimately self-defeating. But it takes more than obvious facts to change an entire economic system.

So what can we do? Where does our lifestyle interlock with campaigning to safeguard our environment? And does caring for the planet really mean going back to a subsistence economy? The answer is that we affect the environment in *everything* we do, and there are many ways in which we can minimize our effects on our environment without having to alter our lifestyles too drastically.

The heart of our economic system is the relationship between the consumer and the producer, between the person who wants something (or is persuaded to want something) and the one who provides it. The overwhelming impression is of control residing in the manufacturer or producer; in fact, the conventional laws of supply and demand demonstrate the opposite. Exercising the right to choose what to buy and what not to buy, particularly when done collectively, makes it possible for individuals to shape both the type of product available and the manner in which it is produced.

SAVING THE RAINFORESTS

In the United States, the demand for cheap beef for hamburgers and other fast foods has directly spurred the destruction of between one-half and two-thirds of Central America's tropical rainforest: some of the most complex and fragile patterns of life ever known totally cleared for cattle pastures that lose their fertility after a few years. Japanese and European demand for cheap tropical hardwoods for furniture, building materials and packaging has accelerated the rapid depletion of similar rainforests in West Africa and South East Asia. To keep operating costs as low as possible, little care is taken during felling, replanting is limited and waste inevitable.

The products of that wasteful clear-felling are all over Britain, most obviously as teak tables or mahogany replacement windows. Stop and think about it before you put in those new windows! There are always alternatives. Friends of the Earth is producing a guide showing which wood products do and don't come from the rainforests. Oak or walnut are every bit as attractive as mahogany.

The eventual cost of destroying the rainforests is far too high: the loss of irreplaceable genetic materials for agriculture, medicine and industry; massive soil erosion and flooding in tropical countries themselves; and the upsetting of global weather patterns, all add up to a mightily expensive bill. Hence the challenge to ecologically-aware consumers to use their influence to persuade international timber companies and hamburger

multinationals to adopt codes of conduct whereby rainforest products are produced sustainably without degrading the environment.

It can be done. As a result of an international consumer boycott initiated by War on Want, the giant agro-combine Nestlés stopped selling powdered milk to mothers in the Third World to feed their babies – a lethal practice in countries where contaminated water is often unavoidable – and in 1984 accepted a Code of Conduct drawn up by the World Health Organization.

EATING

We all do it every day. In other countries people are not so lucky. Many people may remember that Ethiopia was actually exporting melons at the height of its famine. But just think about other 'exotic' foods. Many of the salted peanuts we eat are grown in the Gambia. Peanuts are a major source of protein, yet the people of the Gambia suffer appalling protein deficiency, precisely because the best land is used to grow peanuts and other crops for export.

Peanuts from the Gambia, exotic fruits, coffee, tea, chocolate – the list goes on and on. It's easy to ignore the links, but increasingly there are ways in which we can buy products without relying on the multinational companies responsible for so much of the exploitation of the Third World. Several organizations exist who deal direct with producer groups throughout the world, so that far more of your money ends up with the people who have produced what you're buying. Traidcraft import an enormous range of goods, including Tanzanian coffee. Twin Trading is building up the same kind of network. Aid organizations such as Oxfam bring in goods from the countries which they are aiding.

Home-grown foods are important too. Organically-grown food is a rapidly expanding industry. It is a form of production that deserves our support for many reasons: land and wildlife benefit from not drenching the countryside with chemicals, and there are continuing problems with pesticide residues finding their way into food and vegetables. The more organic food that is sold, the more the price will continue to come down. So if you get the chance, eat organic, and if you can't get organically-grown food, ask your suppliers why not.

Demand for additive-free and organic foods is now so great that advertisers are falling over themselves in the rush to tell us all how 'natural' are their clients' foods. What we as consumers must do is to keep up pressure to ensure that the advertisers' gloss is turned into hard reality.

VISITING THE THIRD WORLD

It's a grim reflection on Westerners to see supposedly caring people arrive for cheap and adventurous holidays in poor countries, and act just like rich tourists. The stereotyped rich American tourist is often unpopular in Europe, yet any Westerner on holiday in India is far, far richer by comparison with the native people than is the American in Europe. Look at how the local people live and conduct their daily affairs, but watch quietly rather than stand there taking photographs.

Any Westerner in the Third World is a target for

beggars and you may feel magnanimous giving a hungry-looking child a couple of coins. But that may be more than the child's parents earn for working all day. Think what that could do to a social system. In some towns you can see the groups of hungry-looking children arriving in the town centres in the morning – why go to school when you can earn ten times what your parents earn by hassling tourists?

Always treat people respectfully and try to understand their lifestyle without being patronizing. Even when you find local customs and lifestyles oppressive or limiting, observe sensitively, remembering that it is their land and culture, not yours. Self-styled teachers and liberators with little experience of the Third World will frustrate themselves and annoy their hosts.

And of course, there's always the environment. Be it Greek islands or Himalayan peaks, it's often a threatened environment put under even more pressure because of tourists like you. So look after it. As the American Sierra Club asks of its members: 'Take nothing but photographs – leave nothing but footprints'.

ANIMALS MATTER

The relationship between humans and other species has been a long and involved one, but whether carnivore, vegetarian or vegan, no one can want to inflict unnecessary pain on animals. There is much dispute about the use of animals in medical research, especially over the almost valueless 'LD50 test' which involves testing any new product for human use on a sample of animals and increasing the dose until 50% of them are dead.

In the short term, one answer is to avoid products from firms that continue to use animals for testing. Beauty Without Cruelty and The Body Shop are two cosmetics firms that do not use any animal experimentation.

DOWN YOUR STREET

If you're going to care about your environment, it makes sense to care about its development. You may not like the proposal to build the hypermarket on green belt land outside town, but one reason it will be going ahead is because the shops down your street are closing down — often, of course, because of competition from the supermarkets.

One way out of this vicious spiral is to shop locally. The hypermarket may be cheaper, but how much money and time are you going to spend getting there? Don't just assume that it's cheaper — take the trouble to work it out. You may find that a surprising amount of material in your local shops is competitively priced when everything is taken into account.

THE AWARE CONSUMER

What democracies need are active participants, informed consumers, openness and involvement. Campaigning organizations spread information and focus attention, but change only comes about when people *demand* it. By insisting on getting involved, people can begin to tap internal resources of strength and fulfilment in exchange for unnecessary material gratification, and thus help to bring about the sustainable society so many yearn for.

RESOURCES

Books:
Des Wilson, *Citizen Action: Taking Action in Your Community* (Longman, 1986)
John McCormick, *The User's Guide to the Environment* (Kogan Page, 1983)

Organizations:

The Consumers' Association (14 Buckingham Street, London WC2) produces the long-standing consumer magazine *Which?*, and can advise on just about any aspect of consumer affairs.

The National Consumer Council (18 Queen Anne's Gate, London SW1) has a network of linked bodies around the country and can also be an invaluable source of advice and information.

If you want to complain try:

The Advertising Standards Authority (Brook House, Torrington Place, London WC1) which covers billboard and magazine advertising.

The Press Council (1 Salisbury Sq., London W1) which deals with complaints about the press and media.

At a local level there are a variety of organizations that can help you. Your local Community Health Council deals with aspects of medical care, but may also be prepared to discuss broader health issues.

Your local council has Environmental Health Officers, and they are the first people to contact about any pollution problem. Similarly the Trading Standards Officers are there to deal with problems over goods on sale.

There are a number of Consumer Councils for industries such as electricity and gas, but all too often they are seriously under-budgeted and seem to have very close links with the organizations they should be watching. However, if they have a regional branch in your area, why not find out what they are doing?

There is one active consumer organization in the electricity industry. They are Consumers Against Nuclear Energy ('We have the power to say no!') who are organizing to withhold a proportion of their electricity bills in protest against nuclear power. Contact them via PO Box 697, London NW1 8YQ.

4.
GOOD HEALTH

When politicians and administrators talk about health issues, it soon becomes clear that they usually mean the provision of facilities for people who are ill or who have hurt themselves. In green terms, however, health is at least as much to do with a life-enhancing environment as about the treatment of illness and accidents. This chapter focuses on environmental approaches to health, using 'environmental' to include social and economic environments, and concentrating on *health* rather than the treatment of disease, whether orthodox or alternative.

Environmental approaches to health have an impressive history; in particular, many of the nineteenth-century public health reforms, such as the separation of sewage from drinking water, provided crucial breakthroughs in caring for people by caring for the environment. Many improvements in health occurred before the advent of modern scientific medicine and were mainly due to a better diet and environment. More recently, the Clean Air Act is another example of an environmental approach. This one piece of legislation alone brought about a massive decrease in the number of respiratory illnesses. Other public health legislation, such as the inspection of food, canteens and cafeterias, has improved health standards in many parts of the world.

PROGRESS?

While much lip service is paid to the promotion of health and the prevention of avoidable accidents and illnesses, an environmental approach to health is still obstinately resisted by powerful people and institutions with a financial interest in pollution and low standards of health and safety. Typically, headlines are given to the dramas of high technology medicine, such as heart transplants. True enough, compared with other industrialized countries Britain certainly has an outstanding problem of heart disease, but heart transplants in no way provide an answer.

Similarly, advertising by the drug industry tends to exaggerate the benefits of its products, even of unarguably valuable drugs such as antibiotics, and to underplay the harmful side-effects, the inflated price of single drugs, and cruel methods of testing.

INDIVIDUAL CHOICE

Today, if and when prevention of accidents and illnesses is given more than lip service, attention tends to be focused on individual lifestyles and personal choices, but the wider environment in which those choices are exercised is normally neglected. Worthwhile contributions to health can indeed be made by individual choices.

Most people could choose to adjust their lives so that they could take regular vigorous exercise, eat healthy food, and not fill their bodies with cigarette smoke and poisonous tar. Given the information now available about the benefits of exercise and a healthy diet, and the proven links between smoking and heart disease or cancer, it's an indication of just how far we've still got to go that so many people still choose to inflict unnecessary risks on themselves. However, a moralizing approach to health education has been notoriously unsuccessful in the past. We need to look at *why* people make unhealthy choices,

41

and concentrate on removing unhealthy influences, as well as educating where there is a lack of knowledge.

Each of these three examples of personal choices about lifestyles also illustrates the importance of the wider environment. Vigorous physical exercise is encouraged, for example, by an environment in which it is both safe and pleasant to cycle, walk or jog, and by leisure centres which are accessible and inexpensive. How easy it is to eat a healthy diet depends, for example, on access to land to grow things, on the local shops, on income levels, on the eating arrangements at work and on how susceptible people are to the ever-present promotion of junk food. Choices about smoking are influenced by advertising and the example set by parents, friends and colleagues.

The basic principles of an environmental approach to health can thus be summarized as: removing or reducing avoidable hazards, and ensuring that the easier choices are the healthy choices. This sort of environmental approach is just one kind of *primary prevention* – preventing problems from ever arising; an example of primary prevention in orthodox medicine is immunization.

HOLISTIC HEALTH

As a simple but reasonably accurate generalization, greens tend to favour alternative or complementary therapies – such as acupuncture or homoeopathy – rather than orthodox medicine, which is typically seen as partial or incomplete in its approach.

One of the most striking characteristics of alternative practitioners is that they usually take much more time to try and understand a patient's problems than orthodox practitioners. First visits will often take an hour or more, compared with the few minutes usually allocated by the average British or American doctor. This extra time is spent looking at their patients 'in the round' – their hopes, burdens and stresses, their lifestyle, the way they relax, and so on.

This comprehensive or 'holistic' approach relates suggestions for an improvement in health directly to the patient's experience of what is wrong. Rather than prescribing tranquillizers to deal with stress, for example, a complementary therapist might look at ways in which the patient could avoid unnecessary stress.

At the same time, environmentalists are usually not totally dismissive of orthodox medicine. In general they would not spurn the use of antibiotics in cases of meningitis, or surgery for a broken limb, appendicitis or cataracts. On the other hand, not all practitioners calling themselves 'alternative' or 'complementary' are compassionate and competent – though most certainly are.

In recent years the enormous gulf between orthodox and alternative practitioners has started to be bridged. Environmentalists welcome this development wholeheartedly.

HEALTHY FOOD

One aspect of lifestyle that many complementary practitioners emphasize is diet, and this is one area of everyday life in which the application of the two basic environmental principles for healthy living can readily be understood.

In terms of avoiding hazards, we can act both as consumers and as workers. Relevant consumer action ranges from individual purchasing choices which support organic methods, to political pressure to increase the pathetic amount of money currently allocated for research into organic methods nationally, and in international organizations such as the UN's Food and Agriculture Organization. We can work for a reduction in toxic herbicides and pesticides which can kill and maim farm workers, partly because they are so poisonous and partly because safeguards regarding their use are so often overlooked or blatantly ignored.

To see how the healthier choices can be made the easier choices, we only need to look at the catering policy of restaurants and canteens. Institutions which serve food can be encouraged to offer people the choice of healthy and appetizing dishes at reasonable prices, but it's not so easy to get them to change their ways. How many factory and office canteens, for instance, still do not serve attractive salads or fresh fruit? Some countries, such as Sweden, reasonably take the view that school meals are important and should foster healthy eating habits. The kind of food that is still served in a lot of hospitals is an appalling reflection of the fact that the National Health Service is still not in the business of promoting health as its first priority.

With wine lakes and mountains of surplus butter and sugar, it is clear that the Common Agricultural Policy has a thing or two to learn about health too! Surplus butter stores in the EEC reached record levels of 1.358 million tonnes in July 1986, and the figures are set to rise in 1987. Some countries are way ahead of others. Norway has set as good example, since 1985, with policies for agriculture, fishing and nutrition which are both health-relevant and responsible in terms of the Third World. For example, by feeding cattle on grass rather than grains, the fat content of meat is reduced, as is the need to import cereals from countries which should primarily be growing food for home consumption.

THE TRANSPORT CONNECTION

6,000 people a year are killed on Britain's roads, and more than a quarter of a million worldwide, not to mention the millions of non-fatal accidents. Many of these are children; more than 15% of child deaths are the result of road accidents. With a transport system so heavily reliant on the motor car, the alternatives of walking and cycling become very dangerous, both in terms of immediate physical danger and the long-term effects of breathing heavily-polluted air. An emphasis on the provision of facilities for private cars at the expense of safe public transport further disadvantages the young, the old and the disabled, detracting from their possibilities of living a truly healthy life.

Action for healthier transport involves pressure on politicians and planners to come up with the right transport policies. From a green perspective, healthier transport patterns would mean actually *reducing* the need for transport (for instance, by promoting local agriculture and industry so that people can live nearer the place where they work), campaigning to hasten the removal of lead and other toxic substances from car exhausts, and supporting the development of integrated transport systems which enhance the quality of people's lives, especially that of the less privileged.

HEALTHY HOUSING

Nearly a hundred thousand families in Britain today have no home to call their own. Many thousands more live in squalid and overcrowded accommodation, with insufficient income and political influence to see any way out. An environmental approach to housing must be concerned with those policies that affect the type, availability and cost of housing. There are many organizations *practically* involved in these concerns, such as Shelter, the Town and Country Planning Association, local housing associations and the Ecology Building Society.

HEALTH AND ENERGY

While the demise of a coal industry prematurely cut down by shortsighted politicians may also be reducing the incidence of silicosis in miners, the wholehearted espousal of nuclear power opens workers to new threats. Avoidable health hazards in the production and consumption of energy include familiar but still very serious problems. In terms of making healthy energy choices the easier choices, the problems range from old people who cannot afford enough heating in winter to avoid hypothermia, to government choices about relative investment in different ways of producing energy.

Local projects concerned with energy conservation, such as Heatwise Glasgow, make practical and immediate contributions to people's health. Not only do they reduce the dangers of hypothermia among the old and other people assisted, they also help to stretch low incomes, to provide socially useful work and to foster constructive relationships between old and young people.

THE ROLE OF THE MASS MEDIA

Mention has already been made of some of the ways in which the mass media have a subtle but very significant effect on people's health by fostering particular ideas about what we mean by 'progress' in health – for instance, by devoting acres of newsprint and hours of broadcasting to hyped-up stories about heart transplant operations, but very little to the causes of coronary heart disease, which has reached epidemic proportions in Britain.

And then there's the thorny question of cigarette advertising. Advertisements for tobacco in the mass

media cost nearly £70 million in the UK alone in 1985.
The heavy expenditure on sponsorship and other forms
of promotion is not publicly known. By comparison, the
Health Education Council has about £2 million a year
to spend on anti-smoking campaigns. Tobacco causes
about 100,000 deaths a year in the UK. Does 'freedom
of the press' really include the freedom of tobacco barons
to buy a sophisticated barrage of propaganda techniques
to persuade people to kill themselves on a massive
scale?

Apart from such glaring health hazards in the mass
media, not least for children, many other advertisements
and other kinds of promotion pressure people towards
unhealthy choices, for instance, in relation to consuming
more alcohol, driving fast cars or guzzling junk food. A
shift towards informative rather than persuasive
advertising would have many advantages in terms of
people's health as well as being sound ecologically. Such
a difficult shift will clearly not come without many more
of the kinds of activities organized by groups such as the
Campaign for Press and Broadcasting Freedom.

UNEMPLOYMENT AND POVERTY

Adverse economic circumstances can sometimes have a
devastating effect on people's health even in a relatively
rich country such as the UK, from hypothermia that
results from poverty, or from homelessness that leads
to a fatal pneumonia.

In recent years, particularly following the publication
in 1980 of the Black Report (*Inequalities in Health*), and
the sharp increase in unemployment and poverty since
the Conservatives came to power in 1979, the damaging
effects of poor socio-economic circumstances on health
have received more attention from medical researchers
– despite government attempts to hide the embarrassing
evidence. Professor Fox and his colleagues at the City
University have shown that unemployment in the UK
in the '70s was associated with death rates that were

about 20% higher than for comparable groups of men in work. The wives of these unemployed men were similarly affected, and other studies have described the damaging effects of involuntary unemployment on the health of children involved.

Because there is so much propaganda about the alleged impossibility of doing anything effective about global economic forces, it is worth remembering that by pursuing quite different investment and training policies from Britain, countries such as Sweden have experienced unemployment levels of less than a quarter of the recent British rates.

A health-oriented interest in the economies of industrialized countries (particularly countries with high unemployment rates, serious resource and pollution problems, and big differences in income), rapidly leads to an interest in 'new economics'. New economics addresses the problems of achieving sustainable and socially just economic development rather than the kind of crude economic 'growth' that is health-damaging as well as being ecologically irresponsible.

THE ARMS RACE

Even from these few examples it is clear that an environmental approach to health is all-embracing. That means making connections of the broadest possible kind. Each and every sector of human activity has profound implications for people's health. For this reason, we find that organizations such as the World Health Organization (WHO), International Physicians for the Prevention of Nuclear War and the British Medical Association regularly attempt to draw public attention to the extreme hazards and extraordinary wastefulness of the arms race. One of WHO's declarations says, for example:

'An acceptable level of health for all the people of the world by the year 2000 can be attained through a fuller and better use of the world's resources, a considerable part of which is now spent on armaments and military conflicts. A genuine policy of independence, peace, détente and disarmament could and should release additional resources that could well be devoted to peaceful aims and in particular to the acceleration of social and economic development of which primary health care, as an essential part, should be allotted its proper share.'

The fact that an environmental approach to health needs to be all-embracing can seem overwhelming if we forget that thousands of people and many organizations are already campaigning for this sort of change. Unlike Canada and the USA, Britain does not yet have a Public Health Association which might give some identity and coherence to these different activities, though such an organization is under discussion.

Meanwhile, we can take comfort from the knowledge that a great deal is already being done to change things, and a comprehensive environmental perspective on public health is growing, nurtured by WHO and many other environmentally-aware groups of people. The last word can be given to the report of the Archbishop of Canterbury's Commission on Urban Priority Areas, *Faith in the City* :

'But if progress is to be made in the large work of promoting healthy living . . . much more attention will have to be paid to the underlying social, economic, housing, environmental and emotional factors which contribute to ill-health. Health care is much more than the treatment of ill-health.'

RESOURCES

Books:
Nancy Milo, *Promoting Public Health*
(Canadian Public Health Association, Ottawa, 1986)
WHO, *Targets for Health for All*
(WHO European Region, 1985)
Stephen Fulder, *The Handbook of Complementary Medicine* (Coronet, 1984)
'Health is Wealth' in Paul Ekins (editor), *The Living Economy* (Routledge and Kegan Paul, 1986)

Magazines:
Radical Community Medicine,
14 Spring Crescent, Portswood, Southampton SO2 1GA
WHO Chronicle and World Health Forum,
WHO, 1121 Geneva 27, Switzerland
Community Health Initiatives Resource Unit Newsletter,
26 Bedford Square, London WC1H 3BU

Organizations:
Stephen Fulder's book (above) gives an excellent list of organizations involved in complementary medicine; the magazine *Radical Community Medicine* (above) contains information on organizations involved in community health.

5.
WHAT'S GOOD FOR YOU . . .

The link between the food we eat and the state of the
environment often seems pretty indirect, although most
of us accept that what we eat affects our health in one
way or another. The health food movement may seem
faddish and its concerns less important than those of the
global environment, but the connections are there. The
food we buy supports methods of food production that
affect not just our own health, but also the health of the
soil and the well-being of people in poorer countries. We
need to find a way of eating which minimizes human and
animal suffering while keeping ourselves and our planet
healthy.

SOWING THE SEEDS OF DISASTER?

Our carrots may look much the same as those eaten by
our grandparents, but the way that 99% of them are
grown in this country today is completely different.
Modern intensive farming methods have only developed
since the last war, before which 'organic farming',
assumed by many to be a new idea, was the only way
of farming known.

Millions of gallons of pesticides and an ever-increasing
amount of nitrogen, potash and phosphate fertilizers are
poured onto the soil every year. These chemicals,

combined with the development of high-technology farming machinery, allows us to produce larger yields with a fraction of the previous workforce – and thus more cheaply.

So far, so good. We get more food for less hard work. An environmentalist, however, will also consider the long-term effects of intensive agriculture upon the soil, upon world resources, upon human health and upon our quality of life.

Agriculture today is depleting the soil, and consequently our food, of vital nutrients. Science is only just discovering the importance of certain trace elements in our diet. Yet every year the proportions of important trace elements in our food crops are decreasing. We just do not know what the long-term effects of this could be on human health. Some of today's crops may be larger, but they also contain more water, have less taste and often contain pesticide residues.

Organic farming is an old tradition, one based on sustainable practices using plants and animals. It balances input with output and, given enough water, converts sunlight into food.

Plants like clover and members of the pea family have root nodules which contain a special type of bacteria. These take up nitrogen from the air and turn it into nitrate fertilizer which is absorbed by the plant. The other major plant nutrients, phospate and potash, are obtained from natural sources such as rocks and seaweed. Forage crops are grazed by farm animals and their manure adds further nutrients to the soil. Animal wastes and crop residues also maintain and increase the soil's organic matter – the humus. This protects soil structure and helps to prevent erosion by wind and water.

Organic agriculture is also based on natural methods of pest control. Mixed farming, free-range livestock systems, a wide variety of crop varieties and promoting natural predators are key factors. These reduce the risks of animal health problems and crop failure due to pests and diseases.

Intensive farming, a largely post-war development, gives top priority to yield. It uses high technology to boost production – from the land, from crops and from animals.

Maximum crop yields depend upon massive inputs of artificial fertilizers. But these, in turn, create ideal conditions for pests and diseases. Fungi thrive in the humid conditions found among a dense leafy canopy. Aphids, often carrying viral diseases, reproduce faster on nitrogen-rich crops. The risk of epidemics increases as more farmers grow ever fewer varieties of crops.

Potentially catastrophic crop losses are averted using chemical pesticides. Some farmers even spray crops before there is any sign of damage; this is called 'insurance spraying'. Further pesticides are used to meet consumer demand for blemish-free products. While scientists develop new crop varieties and new pesticides, modern chemical-intensive farming methods actually encourage the evolution of resistant pests and diseases. Despite pesticides with names such as Commando, Missile, Trident and Avenge, it is an 'arms race' which nature is bound to win.

WORLD HEALTH

Over 500 million people on this planet are severely undernourished, and 40 million die each year from starvation or hunger-related diseases. Meanwhile, people in richer countries wrestle instead with obesity, while their governments accumulate and eventually destroy vast food surpluses.

There are obviously complex political and distributional problems involved in solving the world food crisis, yet the fact remains that animals reared for meat consume 40% of the world's grain – food which could be far better and more efficiently used for feeding people. There is no doubt that a diet high in grains, pulses, vegetables and fruit – with meat as an optional luxury – could feed the present world population. It is equally

beyond doubt that there is just not enough land for everyone in the world to eat what many in the West think of as a normal high-meat diet.

Modern agriculture appears to be cost effective only because the inputs it currently depends on are cheap. But we should really see cost-effectiveness not in terms of money but in terms of energy and raw materials. From this point of view, the Chinese farmer is 5,000% more efficient than the US farmer.

No one is suggesting that we should wind back the clock – modern organic farming combines age-old techniques with the fruits of modern research. But there is no doubt that, unless there is a general shift towards less intensive farming methods, the only way of reducing the EEC's food mountains will be to put some farmers out of business while others carry on just as they do now.

There are certain luxury items of food which are often produced in poorer countries by workers who are badly paid and badly treated – coffee, tea and sugar are examples of these 'cash crops'. In many countries multinational companies now own much of the most fertile land, manage the production, and market the produce – all with little regard for the local people. Organizations such as Traidcraft try to improve the situation by dealing directly with farmers and co-operatives. It is not always in the best long-term interests of the poorer countries to have to use their land for cash crops. Resources are best devoted to meeting local food needs, often by encouraging simple subsistence agriculture.

ANIMAL HEALTH

Every year in Britain, 450 million animals are killed for food. Whether or not we believe that human beings have a moral right to eat animals, we should be aware that animals are now bred, reared and killed in a way which is entirely different from that conjured up by the happy farmyard scenes of our children's books. Battery hens are crammed into overcrowded cages without enough room to flap their wings; dairy cows are robbed of their offspring within a few days of giving birth; many veal calves are kept in tiny crates in virtual darkness.

Keeping large numbers of animals in close confinement increases the risk of diseases. Epidemics are averted by routine dosing of their feed with antibiotics. Even cows' udders are regularly injected to prevent infections. The increasing commonness of resistant strains of salmonella bacteria is probably due to the excessive use of these drugs in agriculture. Antibiotics are also used to increase growth rates. At the same time, intensive livestock systems produce vast quantities of animal wastes, with attendant smells, disposal and water pollution problems.

Neatly clingfilm-wrapped pieces of meat in supermarket fridges keep us neatly removed from any exposure to what really goes on in slaughterhouses and on farms. It may be time to re-evaluate the amounts of meat and dairy produce that we buy, and opt for free-range eggs and smaller amounts of 'organic' meat – meat from animals that are not treated with chemicals and are kept in a humane manner.

HUMAN HEALTH

In 1983, the government's National Advisory Committee on Nutrition Education (NACNE) echoed the conclusions of many other experts the world over in recommending changes in our eating habits. These recommendations included: reducing total fat intake from 38% to 30% of daily calories and saturated fat from 18% to 10%; cutting down on animal-derived proteins and replacing them with proteins from vegetable sources; and increasing fibre intake by 50% by eating more wholegrain cereals, vegetables and fruit. The report also recommended decreasing the intake of salt, sugar and alcohol.

Evidence is now mounting that a refined, low-fibre, high-fat diet is linked to an increased risk for certain diseases, including heart disease, stroke, obesity and particular forms of cancer. Such modern-day epidemics, the so-called 'diseases of affluence', impose a terrible financial burden on our health systems. Any plan for a green future must necessarily promote health-care, rather than sickness-care, by promoting a much healthier national diet.

Although the British government has recently recommended that the labelling of fat and saturated fat in foods should be compulsory, all other nutritional labelling will still be voluntary. Even then, the format suggested only includes fat, saturated fat, protein, carbohydrates and energy – thus making it unnecessary (or even difficult) for manufacturers to give information about other ingredients such as salt and added sugars.

Although the demand for fresh, unprocessed food is growing, many consumers are still influenced mostly by issues of convenience, habit and cost – as well as by advertising and the 'addictive' nature of foods such as salt and sugar. To this end, a variety of food-processing techniques have been developed. These include refining, drying, canning, freezing and the use of chemical additives as preservatives, flavourings and colourings.

What makes money for the food producers is not always

best for our health. We assume that the government would act to stop any practices which are actually harmful, but the influential nature of the food industry means that this does not always occur. In fact, so resistant is the system to change that the NACNE report referred to above was actually 'held up' in the Ministry of Agriculture for two years – because of its far-reaching implications. Issues such as the labelling of food, additives, pesticides in food and the introduction of new preservation techniques (such as food irradiation) often have to be taken up by public interest groups.

SO WHAT'S WRONG WITH OUR FOOD?

The nutritional implications of the techniques mentioned above can be quite devastating. The refining of wheat-grain to make white flour results in a dramatic loss of mineral, vitamin and fibre content – up to 84% of some nutrients. These then have to be replaced in the flour manufacturing process. The freezing of vegetables is nutritionally preferable to canning, but both processes cause a loss of nutritional value. An estimated 3,850 different additives are currently permitted for use in food; in 1984 the average consumer ate 2.5 kg of them!

Britain has the weakest set of food additive regulations of all the industrialized countries. Not all the additives in use have been properly tested, and many of the unavoidable cocktails of additives in use have never been tested. Some cause observable reactions such as allergies, but the long-term health effects of many others are simply not known. All additives (except flavourings) are now legally required to be indicated on the food label with the appropriate E number, and can be looked up in one of the additive directories now available.

We thus have some element of choice about which additives to eat – a choice which is not available for pesticide residues. In 1984 a survey by the Association of Public Analysts discovered that one-third of all fruit and vegetables tested had detectable chemical residues – some, including DDT, which had theoretically been banned.

Friends of the Earth is campaigning against the overuse and misuse of pesticides, and in particular against aerial spraying. This method of application contributes to the hundreds of cases reported every year of members of the public who have been sprayed with or contaminated by these chemicals. Incidents of this kind are published in FoE's regular Pesticide Incidents Reports. Such incidents often lead to serious and persistent health problems, which is even more worrying when at least 40 of the chemicals permitted for regular use have been linked with cancer; 89 with allergies or skin irritation; 61 with mutagenic effects; and 31 with birth defects.

WHO'D BE A CARNIVORE?

If you do eat meat, then eat less and cut off the fat! Meat is high in saturated fat – and there is evidence to show that pesticide residues accumulate especially in the fat of the animal. A typical high-meat, low-fibre Western diet has been linked with cancer of the colon and rectum. The hormones and antibiotics used in animal farming affect humans too: overuse of antibiotics can lead to drug-resistant bacteria developing which can strike at both humans and animals. 80% of the chicken carcasses sold in shops are estimated to be infected with salmonella bacteria. This potentially lethal bug must be killed by cooking.

The hormones used in farming are present in our meat. Nitrites are also routinely added to cured meats, despite the possible link with cancer. There is also a potentially dangerous build-up of nitrates in our environment.

Liver and kidneys are high in nutrients, but are also the parts of the animals' bodies which concentrate the chemical residues. Fish from the sea have not had their diets meddled with, but sometimes contain high levels of toxic heavy metals and chemical residues from the steady stream of pollutants poured into our coastal waters.

It is not easy at first to change our shopping and eating habits, but there is no doubt that food and diet are *real* environmental issues.

RESOURCES

There are many different ways in which you can help to bring about change and improve your own health. The most important is through your power as a consumer. If your local shops and supermarkets do not stock what you wish to buy, then ask them to consider doing so. Help to create the demand that will make for a healthier and more compassionate world. There are many organizations listed below who can provide you with further information and suggestions for actions and campaigns. (NB. If you write for information, please send a s.a.e.)

ORGANIC FOODS

Organic vegetables, fruit, flour/grain and meats are becoming increasingly available. Safeway supermarkets stock organic vegetables and fruit and other chains are following suit. Many restaurants are now using organic ingredients. Members of the Soil Association can check the credentials of suppliers in the Association's guide. Look for their seal of approval on food products. Those who grow their own produce can obtain information on how to grow organically from the addresses below:

Organizations:
The Henry Doubleday Research Association (The National Centre for Organic Gardening, Ryton-on-Dunsmore, Coventry CV8 3LG; tel. 0203 303517). Demonstration centre open to visitors, membership, information, books, leaflets.
The Soil Association (86 Colston Street, Bristol BS1 5BB; tel. 0272 290661). Membership, information, books, leaflets.

Books:
A Gear, *The New Organic Food Guide* (Dent, 1987) Obtainable from bookshops or Henry Doubleday Research Association. Detailed critique of intensive

farming and a guide to obtaining organic produce.
C. Johnstone, *The Real Food Shop and Restaurant Guide*
(Ebury, 1985).

HEALTHY EATING

You may wish to cut down on meat and dairy produce
in your diet and to eat more fresh wholefoods. Avoid
additives and foods that are wastefully overwrapped.
Experiment with new ways of cooking wholefood
ingredients – they can be really delicious!

Organizations:

The McCarrison Society (c/o Wholefood, 24 Paddington
Street, London W1M 4DR). Membership, lectures,
information, books, research, campaigning.
The London Food Commission (PO Box 291, London
N5 1DU). Independent research, advice and training
organization. Membership, newspaper, reports,
publications (including information on additives,
pesticides, nitrates, labelling and irradiation).
ECOROPA (Crickhowell, Powys, Wales NP8 1TA).
Leaflets on additives, diet, cancer. Books,
membership.
The Vegetarian Society (Parkdale, Dunham Road,
Altrincham, Cheshire; tel. 061 928 0793). Membership,
direct action, books, cookery courses. Publishes *The
International Vegetarian Handbook*.
The Vegan Society (33-35 George Street, Oxford
OX1 2AY; tel 0865 722166). Membership, local groups,
books, leaflets, information.

Books:

G. Cannon and C. Walker, *The Food Scandal*
(Century, 1984)
The British Dietetic Association, *The Great British Diet*
(Century, 1985)
J. Erlichman, *Gluttons for Punishment*
(Penguin, 1986)

M. Hanssen, *E for Additives*
  (Thorsons, 1984)
Dr E. Millstone, *Food Additives – taking the lid off
what we eat* (Penguin, 1986)

Cookbooks:
Dr S. Gibson *et al, Cook Yourself a Favour*
  (Thorsons/Vegetarian Society, 1986)
E. Buchman Ewald, *Recipes for a Small Planet*
  (Ballantine, 1973)

FOOD, WORLD HUNGER AND RESOURCES

Organizations:
Oxfam (274 Banbury Road, Oxford OX2 7DZ; tel. 0865
  56777). Campaigns (including 'Hungry for Change'),
  local activities, publications, development and relief
  work abroad.
World Development Movement (Bedford Chambers,
  London WC2E 8HA; tel. 01-836 3672). Membership,
  local groups, publications, information.
Christian Aid (PO Box 1, London SW9 8BH; tel. 01-733
  5500). Newspaper, publications, educational materials,
  development work abroad.

Books:
F. Moore Lappé and J. Collins, *Food First – A new action
  plan to break the famine trap* (Abaacus, 1982)
J. Wynne Tyson, *Food for a Future* (Centaur, 1975)
R. Waller, *The Agricultural Balance Sheet*
  (Green Alliance, 1982). Available from the Green
  Alliance (60 Chandos Place, London WC2N 4HG)

FACTORY FARMING

The organizations listed opposite work in non-violent
ways to bring about the end of cruelty to animals in
farming. Contact them for details of direct action and
other campaigning activities.

Organizations:

Animal Aid (7 Castle Street, Tonbridge, Kent TN9 1BH; tel. 0732 364546). Membership, local groups, literature, campaigns, educational material.

Compassion in World Farming (20 Lavant Street, Petersfield, Hants GU32 3EW; tel. 0730 64208). Membership, local groups, newsletters, direct actions, leaflets, educational materials.

The Vegetarian Society (address on page 61).

The Vegan Society (address on page 61).

Books:

M. Gold, *Assault and Battery*
(Pluto Press, 1983)

OTHER CAMPAIGNS AND ISSUES

Third World Products:

Traidcraft, Kingsway, Gateshead, Newcastle-upon-Tyne NE11 0NE.

Twin Trading, 345 Goswell Road, London EC1V 7JT (Wholesale enquiries only).

Labelling:

The Ministry of Agriculture's proposals are thought by many to be inadequate. Campaign for *full nutritional labelling* to be compulsory (including items outside the proposed format such as salt and sugars). Write to the major food companies, the Minister of Agriculture and your MP and tell them what you think. Information on the issues can be obtained form the London Food Commission (address on page 61).

Pesticides:

Contact Friends of the Earth for up-to-date details of the Pesticides and Pesticide-Free Food Campaigns – and for details of current legislation on aerial spraying and permitted food residue levels.

The London Food Commission also has useful information (address on page 61).
Friends of the Earth, 377 City Road, London EC1V 1NA; tel. 01-837 0731).

Additives:
Send a s.a.e. to FACT (The Food Additives Campaign Team) for details of how to help.
Address: 25 Horsell Road, London N5 1XL.

Food irradiation:
The British government has approved, in principle, the introduction of food irradiation (subjecting food to radiation in order to preserve it). However, a recent deluge of letters to the DHSS has caused them to extend their consultative deadline. Write to the London Food Commission for their information and publications; write to your MP, food companies and supermarkets and make them aware of your views. If the consumer does not want to buy food that has been irradiated, then it will never be commercially viable!

6.
WEALTH FROM WASTE

One of the basic laws of nature is that nothing actually disappears when it is thrown away – and this is what lies at the root of many of the environmental problems we experience today. Every year in Britain, over 23 million tonnes of household and commercial waste are thrown away. This prodigious annual amount of waste has grown enormously in recent years.

More and more material is designed to be thrown away immediately, often in the form of complex packaging. Many manufactured items are designed to have a very short lifespan – just think of magazines and newspapers – and a great deal of time and energy is put into persuading consumers to throw away their old possessions and buy new ones. Much of this so-called 'waste' contains potentially valuable material which, if separated, could be recycled rather than thrown away.

WHY RECYCLE?

A great deal could be done about waste by not creating it in the first place, by buying wisely and consuming wisely, but once the 'waste' does exist, a great many useful things can be done with it. Recycling means putting waste back into productive use, and waste can be recycled in many ways – for example, waste paper can be used to make recycled paper, as the basis for compost, to make a fuel, or burnt in an incinerator to recover the heat of its combustion.

Many of the advantages of recycling are fairly obvious. The more we use recycled materials, the less we need to use 'virgin' raw materials. Because the 'waste' has already been processed, it usually uses less energy to create recycled products than to produce the same products from raw materials. Recycling creates more jobs than waste dumping, and at the same time reduces environmental damage caused by indiscriminate dumping.

Despite these potential benefits, Britain still has no national policy on recycling. To quote the government's own 1984 Trade and Industry Department *Wealth of Waste* report, 'opportunities for recycling and resource recovery . . . are not exploited as vigorously in the UK as they might be'.

There's still a great deal the individual can do, and the strength of consumer pressure should not be underestimated. Similarly, pressure applied on local authorities can help to increase the opportunities available for recycling materials. Many local authority sites now include facilities such as bottle banks, and in some areas recycling centres are in operation.

Households can reduce unnecessary waste by remembering two basic principles:

- before you buy something, ask yourself if you really need it
- before you throw something away, consider whether there is any alternative use for it.

PAPER

In Britain, we each consume an average of 130 kg of paper every year – the equivalent of between one and two trees per person, and amounting to over 7.7 million tonnes. Paper products use approximately 35% of the world's annual commercial wood harvest – this figure is predicted to rise to 50% by the year 2000. At present, only 25% of the world's paper is recycled, although there is no technical or economic reason why this figure could not be doubled by the end of this century.

The British Paper and Board Industry Federation have estimated that the UK could save over £400 million annually (in terms of imports of wood pulp and finished products) if greater use could be made of waste paper. About 38% of the paper and board used in Britain is recycled. The UK waste paper industry suffers from severe competition from pulp-rich countries, and subsidies on imported papers have placed recycled paper at an economic disadvantage.

The key to this problem is to increase the use of recycled paper by creating a demand for it. An ideal target here is central and local government, as both are large users of paper.

Other things you can do to save paper include:

- supporting local paper recycling schemes run by community groups; newspapers and magazines are the most frequently collected grades
- contacting the local council for details of any schemes they might operate, though the fluctuating price of waste paper on the open market has increased the

instability of the waste paper industry and many local authorities have found it uneconomic to collect paper on a door-to-door basis

- if the market appears good, you could start a collection. Friends of the Earth can provide advice on this

- buying and using recycled paper products wherever possible and encouraging others to do so. A list of stockists is available from FoE

- envelopes can be re-used if carefully opened; special re-use stickers can be purchased from FoE and elsewhere

- paper bags can be used again and again. Bags and egg boxes are usually welcomed by wholefood shops.

GLASS

Every year over six billion glass bottles and jars are used in Britain. While the main components of glass (sand, limestone and soda ash) are relatively cheap and plentiful, their quarrying has a significant impact on the environment.

Every tonne of cullet (broken glass) used in the glass-making process saves the equivalent of 150 litres of oil and replaces 1.2 tonnes of raw materials. Put another way, this is a 25% saving of the total energy used to produce glass.

Friends of the Earth has been campaigning for years for legislation to make all bottles returnable, and of a standard size and shape to help re-use. The strong commercial interests of the packaging and retailing industries defeated this move, and today returnable bottles are increasingly hard to find, especially in large retail outlets. However, four out of every five containers are potentially re-fillable, made up for the most part of milk bottles and all those bottles from licensed premises.

Bottle banks were introduced by the Glass

Manufacturers' Federation in 1977, partly as a response to growing pressure concerning non-returnable bottles. In 1985, 210,000 tonnes of cullet were recycled – still a relatively low amount compared to other European countries. A major problem is that Britain has just 2,500 banks for 55 million people, compared to Holland's 10,000 banks for a population of 14 million.

Although the Glass Manufacturers' Federation has made a commitment to try to double the number of bottle banks in Britain over the next five years, we still have some way to go in developing successful resource-recovery schemes. It is difficult to make direct comparisons between different countries since each has different kinds of waste and varying options for waste disposal. For example, while the UK has plenty of landfill sites, many European countries do not, and so have legislated against the widespread use of non-returnable containers.

In addition, waste disposal companies on the Continent are often private contractors who have recognized the value of recycling – the Netherlands and Germany are examples here. Another factor that has to be considered is the arrival of the plastic polyethylene terepthalate (PET) bottle, which has had a significant impact on the beverage container industry. In Germany PET bottles are still allowed, but a deposit is imposed to ensure retrieval for recycling.

Where glass containers are still in widespread use, countries such as the Netherlands are encouraging moves for the standardization of bottles and for distinctive marking of refillable containers. Glass recycling is generally high in European countries, with over 3 million tonnes of cullet recycled in 1985. In Denmark the sale of non-refillable soft drinks containers is prohibited, while nine states in the USA currently operate successful deposit legislation controls.

Things you can do to help include:

- support your local bottle bank. Although they have encouraged the use of the one-trip bottle, they are preferable to throwing the bottles in the dustbin. Observe the bottle bank code – metal caps can cause furnace damage
- encourage your local authority (if they operate the bank) to donate the proceeds to local community projects, creating further incentives to recycle
- if there is no bottle bank in your area, contact your local councillor and MP to find out why. Contact the cleansing waste disposal section of the council. Write a letter to your local paper. Advice can be obtained from the Glass Manufacturers' Federation
- support companies that still use returnable bottles – in the British soft drinks market, that's Corona and R.J. Whites. Don't forget to return them
- buy milk in bottles rather than cartons. Do not put milk bottles in bottle banks
- re-use bottles and jars wherever possible; local wholefood shops often need jars.

METALS

Iron, steel, tin, copper and aluminium are the most easily recycled metals. Ferrous scrap recovery (iron and steel) is a well-established business in Britain. For disposal of quantities of these materials, scrap metal merchants can be found in the Yellow Pages.

In 1984 over 2 billion food and drink cans were produced in the UK, made either from all-aluminium or aluminium tin-plated steel for drinks cans, and tin plate for food cans. Potentially all of these cans could be recycled, the main problem being collection in sufficient quantities.

An aluminium container is the most energy-intensive form of packaging and therefore should be recycled. It takes 31 barrels of oil (or energy equivalent) to make 1 tonne of aluminium from imported bauxite ore, compared with only 2 barrels of oil when aluminium scrap is used. Of the 3.8 billion cans used for drinks packaging annually, approximately half are pure aluminium. Given their scrap value, it's hardly surprising that an increasing number of collection schemes are now being set up.

What you can to do to help:
- if Save-a-Can skips exist in your area, use them. They take all types of cans
- you can separate your aluminium cans (aluminium is non-magnetic), and use aluminium can schemes as a way of raising funds. FoE will happily provide details
- avoid buying aerosols
- old fridges, cookers etc. should not be dumped, but taken to civic amenity sites. Recycling workshops can also refurbish these articles.

PLASTICS

Plastics have replaced many manufacturing materials once commonly used. While they are suitable for many purposes, two major problems exist at the household level. Once mixed with other materials, plastics cannot be recycled; and because they are not 'biodegradable' (capable of being decomposed by living matter), they do not rot away when buried.

About thirty different plastics are in everyday use, and

it is this mixture, together with the problems caused by the sheer volume of plastics in use, which leads the British Plastics Federation to advise people not to consider plastic recycling schemes. To collect a tonne of polystyrene would require 250,000 vending cups, and you'd need about 300,000 plastis carrier bags for a tonne of polyethylene!

Many problems still surround the use of biodegradable plastics, and they have only been used on a limited scale in Britain. Although some plastics, particularly those used in packaging, are advertised as biodegradable, this is only a matter of degree. Some plastics which bear the label 'biodegradable' actually release undesirable by-products into the environment, so it is best to steer clear of plastics as far as you can.

The best policy is to avoid the use of plastics wherever possible. Small items, such as yoghurt pots, can have a variety of household uses, and they can always be donated to a local playgroup.

OIL

Unfortunately, many motorists are still unaware that used sump oil from DIY oil changes can be recycled if it is returned to garages or civic amenity sites.

At present 100,000 tonnes of oil is unaccounted for, and evidence points to a high rate of illegal dumping or pouring down drains. A gallon of oil down the drain can cause blockages and pollution problems; just that small amount has the capacity to form a visible film over four acres of water. If you have oil to dispose of, enquire whether your local garage will accept oil, or find out if your local authority has set up any collection schemes.

TEXTILES

Good quality secondhand clothes, blankets and other furnishings can be re-used if sold to a dealer or donated to charities such as Oxfam or the Salvation Army. Lower quality materials end up as mixed rags which are separated and used for a variety of purposes including wiping cloths, upholstery stuffing and woollen spun cloth.

Off-cuts of new materials from manufacturing industries can be useful for children's playgroups or scrap-store projects.

ORGANIC WASTE

A fair proportion of household waste can be composted to create garden fertilizer. Vegetable peelings, tea leaves and garden waste, such as grass clippings, can all be used. Advice leaflets are available from the Henry Doubleday Research Association (see page 60) and a variety of compost bins can be brought, including a Tumbler which produces compost in only 21 days.

BITS AND BOBS

A variety of other materials can be reclaimed and usefully re-used (don't forget timber offcuts!).

Items such as old stamps, coins, aluminium foil and ring-pulls are welcomed by charities for fundraising (contact FoE for a list) whilst old books, clothes, household items and toys can be donated to charity shops or jumble sales.

EXCESSIVE PACKAGING

Ever since Friends of the Earth dumped 1,500 non-returnable bottles on the doorstep of Schweppes in 1971, the issue of one-trip packaging has remained a target for consumer pressure.

In 1982, packaging costs in the UK amounted to £3,300 million — equivalent to £3.10 per week for each of the 20.5 million households. Approximately 28% of the contents of an average dustbin is made up of discarded packaging. As well as being big business, the industry is very energy-intensive, with product advertising fostering the throwaway mentality by stressing consumer convenience.

While some packaging is undoubtedly essential, the trend towards the excessive use of materials is escalating. The packaging industry *is* subject to a voluntary code of conduct, but there are no legal means of enforcing packaging standards. The code asks that excessive or deceptive packaging should be avoided by the manufacturers, and that packaging design needs to take into account possible wastage of resources and the subsequent re-use or recycling of the material. This code of conduct in blatantly disregarded by many manufacturers and retailers.

Concern within the European Community over the increasing numbers of beverage containers being thrown away led to the eventual adoption in June 1985 of the EEC Directive on Containers of Liquids for Human Consumption. The Directive recommends that the proportion of non-returnable containers is reduced, and that efficient methods of collecting non-returnable containers (glass, metal, plastic etc.) should be investigated. In addition, the Directive requires that careful attention be paid to the design of packaging to make recycling easier, and that a consumer education programme into the benefits of re-use/recycling should be implemented.

For the first time, the packaging industry will be forced to consider seriously the environmental impact of their products. In Britain, the Directive is to be implemented by voluntary controls – so progress will have to be monitored very closely indeed. Although the Directive only refers to drinks containers, it is hoped that there may be some spin-off into other sections of the industry.

What you can do to help:

- always avoid pre-packaged goods wherever possible, and if you do have to buy an over-packaged article, you can unwrap the goods at the sales point and hand the material back to the shop
- if you feel a product is over-packaged, complain! This can be done in person or by letter to the shopkeeper, supermarket manager, manufacturer, local newspaper, your local MP, or the Packaging Council (c/o INCPEN, College House, Great Peter Street, London SW1P 3NQ). Encourage others to complain in particular cases – do not underestimate consumer power! If you feel the packaging is deceptive, you could voice your complaint to the Institute of Trading Standards (Metropolitan House, 37 Victoria Avenue, Southend-on-Sea, Essex SS2 6DA).
- avoid unnecessary bags (particularly plastic carrier bags) and remember to take a shopping bag with you
- some retail outlets use 100% recycled paper packaging, such as the Treesaver Bags. Congratulate them
- try to buy goods in bulk, rather than in small, individually packaged quantities
- encourage local councils to provide adequate litter bins, especially in heavily-frequented areas. Check to make sure they are emptied regularly. Never drop litter yourself! If sponsorship schemes are not already operating, suggest this idea to the council. Local shops can sponsor a litter bin as a way of contributing to the care of the local environment and promoting a sense of civic pride in the area.

RESOURCES

Books:
FoE/Earth Resources Research, *Material Gains: Reclamation, Recycling and Reuse* (1979, shortly to be updated)
Worldwatch, *Materials Recycling: The Virtue of Necessity* (Worldwatch Paper No. 56, available from Conservation Books, 228 London Road, Reading RG6 1AH)

Organizations:
GENERAL
National Agency for Litter Abatement,
    Bostel House, 37 West Street, Brighton, Sussex BN1 2RE
FoE,
    377 City Road, London EC1V 1NA
    (Send s.a.e. for recycled paper product list, and list of charities which can use recycled materials.)

PAPER
British Paper and Board Industry Federation,
    3 Plough Place, Fetter Place, London EC4
British Waste Paper Association,
    Highgate House, 214 High Street, Guildford, Surrey GU1 3JB

GLASS
The Glass Manufacturers' Federation,
    19 Portland Place, London W1N 4BH

METAL
The Canmakers' Information Service,
    36 Grosvenor Gardens, London SW1
Save-a-Can
    Queen's House, Forbury Road, Reading RG1 3JH
The Aluminium Federation,
    Broadway House, Calthorpe Road, Birmingham B15

7.
HOMING IN ON ENERGY

Every year, each person in the Western world uses a quantity of energy (mostly in the form of electricity, gas, petroleum products and solid fuel) equivalent to the burning of six tonnes of coal. Not only does this cost a lot of money; it has a direct impact on the environment in the form of spoil tips, nuclear waste dumping, acid rain from power stations and the effect of electricity pylons on the countryside. Obviously the more we can reduce our demand for energy, the more money we save *and* the less damage we do to our surroundings.

It is also important to be aware of the sources of our energy, and the implications of those different sources. Many forms of energy production use resources which cannot be replaced, such as coal and oil. Nuclear energy, until recently heralded as the panacea of the energy industry, has been shown to have potentially disastrous side-effects, and very many people are concerned about the consequences of a nuclear future. Alternative sources of energy are now being developed which use 'renewable' resources – ways of producing power which will not run out, and which have a much smaller impact on the environment, such as hydro-electricity, wind power, solar panels, tidal power, wave power, and biomass and geothermal energy.

There are many ways in which we can reduce consumption without dramatically affecting our lifestyle. We are lucky to have this choice – a choice which many

people around the world simply don't have. The average
person in Britain uses 320 times as much energy as the
average Nepalese, more than fifty times as much as the
average Kenyan, and three times as much as someone
from Argentina or Mexico. Even compared to developed
nations such as Denmark and Spain, we use between 10%
and 40% more energy.

Nearly 70% of the energy we use in the home is for
heating rooms. This is called space heating. A further
17% is used to produce hot water. The remainder is for
cooking (around 7%), and for electrical appliances such
as lights, fridges and freezers, TVs and the like. How
many of us can remember being told by our parents to
'turn off the lights' in order to save electricity? In reality,
such energy saving measures have only a small potential
to reduce our bills, since lights only use about 1½% of
the total energy in the house. But it's the *attitude* that
counts, and even the smallest of measures is important
when it comes to counteracting the chronic wastefulness
of the way we live.

TIME FOR NEW SOLUTIONS?

When we pay our quarterly bills to the electricity and
gas boards, we expect a range of services in return. We
expect power at the flick of a switch and instant heat
24 hours a day. But energy in the home is expensive. The
average home in Britain costs between £300 and £400
every year in energy. Some families spend almost as much
on heating as they do on food.

For many it is too much – nearly 100,000 electricity
consumers a year are disconnected because they have
failed to pay their bills. A further 230,000 people on social
security have fuel payments made directly to the gas and
electricity boards because of financial difficulties. In
extreme cases, the costs of trying to save on heating bills
can lead to death from hypothermia, the incidence of
which has increased significantly since the early 1970s.
Between 1979 and 1984, an average of 1,230 people have

died every year. The central cause of these problems is that a high proportion of our housing is old, poorly insulated and insufficiently heated.

Nearly 75% of our housing stock was built before 1965, and was not subject to any minimum insulating or heating standards. Around 40% of housing is of solid wall construction, which loses heat at more than three times the rate of the walls of new houses. Nearly 80% of our lofts have less than 1 cm of insulation, well below the level which is now cost effective and required by the government for new homes. Our homes are also relatively draughty, with an average air-change rate of around 1.5 per hour, twice that of buildings built after the war. Around 35% of all homes have no central heating, including over four million homes in the local authority and privately rented sector. As a result an estimated 2½ million homes in England and Wales suffer from condensation and dampness.

The recognition that we need not live with this state of affairs is beginning to have far-reaching consequences. In Salford and Milton Keynes, for example, nearly 300 super-insulated homes have been built. The space and water heating bills for these houses range from £70 to

£200 per year. The homes are warmer than average, comfortable to live in and draught-free.

INSULATION

It would be technically possible to reduce our energy needs by as much as two-thirds by improving the efficiency with which we use energy. A lot of this saving can be achieved by making full use of the heat we generate to keep ourselves warm, rather than losing it through draughty doors and windows, up chimneys, and through thin walls and ceilings. The prevention of this loss – the 'wrapping up warmly' of buildings – is called insulation.

Draughtstripping is one of the simplest and cheapest ways of saving energy. Rubber and plastic seals around doors, windows, cracks in floorboards and walls, old fireplaces and letterboxes can stop draughts sucking out heat. Costs for a whole house range from £30 to £60. This can sometimes be paid back in less than a year.

Those currently on supplementary benefit can apply to the DHSS for a 'single payment' to cover this cost. Whilst this doesn't pay for labour, there are now more than 250 schemes operated by Neighbourhood Energy Action (NEA) which can help. These schemes generally use high quality draughtstripping materials bought at discounts through bulk buying.

If you want to carry out the work yourself, ask for advice on the best materials. Try and avoid the cheap sticky-backed foam often sold in hardware shops, since this generally has a short life.

Hot water tanks are usually sold with an insulation jacket. If not, jackets can be bought for £6 to £10 and are easily fitted. They usually pay back this cost within a few months.

Loft insulation is more expensive, between £100 and £250 depending on the type of house. A range of materials can be used, such as fibreglass, mineral wool and loose granular fill. Grants are available from your local authority covering 65% of the total cost including labour, or 90% if you are a pensioner or suffer from ill-health. 'Topping-up' grants are also available for lofts which have ½ cm of insulation or less. Do make sure that you get permission for a grant *before* carrying out the work, and use gloves, old overalls and a simple mask because it can be very messy in a loft. Once again, your local NEA scheme can help with labour if you are a pensioner or on supplementary benefit.

Wall insulation includes cavity insulation, or solid wall insulation fitted either to the inside or outside of the wall. Materials include polystyrene balls, mineral fibre, polystyrene blocks or foam. There has been some concern over the gases given off by urea fomaldehyde foam, so it is probably better to avoid this.

Costs range from £250 to £400 for cavity wall insulation, and from £800 to £2000 for solid wall insulation. Pay-back times are two to eight years for the former, and six to forty years for the latter. No grants are available at present, and solid wall insulation is only really cost effective if you or the local council is carrying out rehabilitation work at the same time.

Commercial **double-glazing** is not really an effective energy conservation measure, since it is quite expensive and may take between 15 and 60 years to pay back the costs. It does of course provide other benefits such as reduced noise, and is a good idea if you are fitting new windows anyway. Fitting secondary glazing behind your present windows is also relatively cheap. In order of priorities, double glazing only makes sense if you have carried out the other insulation measures first.

LIGHTING, HEATING AND APPLIANCES

Remember those lights we were all told to switch off? Did you know that modern lighting systems are available which use less than a fifth of the energy of the old light bulbs? These are based on fluorescent tubes, and can be adapted to fit straight on to the old fittings. While they cost a bit more, they soon pay for themselves as they last longer and use much less electricity.

Choosing energy-efficient central heating boilers and appliances such as kettles and fridges is more difficult, because it is often hard to work out how much energy they use. Many countries sell appliances with energy labels attached, but with the exception of the Eastern Electricity Board, these are not available in Britain. There are a number of things you can sensibly do, however:

- use kettles which switch off automatically, particularly the tall ones which don't need to boil a full kettle every time
- use pressure cookers to cut cooking times
- use gas and electric cookers which allow you to use only part of the grill or cooking ring.

CONTROLS

Many homes have poor temperature controls for radiators. This means that different rooms are either overheated or underheated. Individual thermostats costing between £10 and £12 can be fitted to all radiators, allowing easy control in all rooms. If you have a thermostat for your central heating system, make sure it is in the living room and not in the hall or the kitchen.

Electronic timers are also a great help in controlling heat. They can either be part of the central heating system or fitted at each electric socket to control individual heaters. Make sure you adjust the timers when warmer weather arrives or before you go on holiday.

DISTRICT HEATING SYSTEMS

More energy is lost from our power stations than is provided by North Sea gas every year. Stations which produce electricity, but also make use of the heat which is normally wasted, are called Combined Heat and Power

(CHP) stations. Many countries in the world use CHP in a big way. In Denmark, 32% of the heat used in homes comes from either CHP or District Heating (DH) systems, producing heat for groups of houses from a central boiler. In Britain, the figure is 3%.

Many local authorities now want to build CHP schemes, but the gas and electricity boards, and the government, have been lukewarm about the idea. There is now a growing campaign to bring CHP to our major cities. Not only would it save energy, but it would generate employment in the inner cities and help to upgrade some of our poorer housing stock.

District Heating schemes have sometimes suffered in the past from bad design and poor metering and control. Users have often been left with no sources of heat as boilers have broken down, or have been either too hot or too cold with no way of altering this except by opening windows or putting on additional electric fires. More modern systems have solved most of these problems.

ALTERNATIVE ENERGY SOURCES

Fossil fuels and uranium for nuclear power are finite. They also create a range of environmental problems, such as pollution and the risk of accidents. Renewable energy sources are one way of reducing these problems. At present, solar heating, wind-powered electricity or biogas from organic wastes can be more expensive than conventional sources. The costs are coming down, however, and in the future they have a huge potential.

Passive solar heating involves putting large south-facing windows or conservatories on houses. The Department of Energy now regard passive solar energy as economic. The real problem is a lack of information and understanding by architects, builders and consumers. Despite this, over 400 passive solar houses have now been built, many in the new town of Milton Keynes. The additional features add only marginally to the costs, but can contribute up to one-third of the heating needs of the home.

Conservatories are now very popular. Not only do they provide a pleasant additional living space, but they can heat the rest of the house, particularly if vents in the walls are made to pass this heat into other rooms.

It's a Conservatory Party Conference...

In some parts the world, solar water heating systems are both advanced and relatively cheap. In other countries, including Britain, the cost of solar water heating is still prohibitive, though big savings could be made if the components were manufactured on a large scale.

NEW ENERGY SOURCES

Small-scale **wind generators** are becoming more easily available. Linked with heavy-duty batteries, they can provide all the power needed for lights and other appliances. For farms, isolated houses or country cottages, particularly those not linked to the electricity grid, they can be a very realistic choice. However, many homes are unsuitable for wind generators, either because the area is not windy enough, or gardens are too small.

Solar electric cells are often used in watches and calculators. For individual homes, they remain much too expensive. If costs fall rapidly in the next ten years, as new techniques are developed, they could be realistic sources of power in the future.

Wave and tidal power are only really suitable on a large scale. Tidal power is particularly attractive in Britain, as six of our major estuaries could provide 20% of our current electricity consumption. Careful studies into the effects of tidal barrages on natural ecosystems need to be carried out before building such schemes.

Heat pumps and mini-power stations (known in the business as 'mini-chips') are available now to provide heat and power. They make a lot of sense for group heating schemes or small businesses, but are still too expensive for individual homes.

Heat pumps use heat from the ground or the air around us, and upgrade it to produce two to three times the energy used. Mini-chips are, in effect, mini-CHP stations. Using car or industrial engines, they can operate at an efficiency of more than 80%. Unlike large power stations, which take eight to ten years to build, mini-chips can be in operation within a few weeks or months.

Biogas is produced when organic waste decomposes in a 'digester', producing a gas suitable for cooking, plus a rich fertilizer. Some homes in Denmark have these connected to sewage systems, with supplements from chicken and cow manure. Special toilets, called Clivius toilets, are in use throughout the world. These decompose sewage without producing the gas.

A simple way of using organic waste is, of course, to compost it in the garden. The heat produced in a compost heap helps to break down the wastes into a rich manure for the soil.

TAKING ON THE NUCLEAR JUGGERNAUT

These new sources of energy could clearly have a significant impact on our lives in the near future. Unfortunately, the shortsightedness of current policies means that the vast majority of energy investment is

going into nuclear power – Britain spent over £300
million on it last year, compared with just £14 million
on researching new sources.

Several times in the last few years, people have woken
up to find that their home town or village is suddenly
front page news as a result of a government proposal to
site a nuclear waste dump or even a nuclear power station
on their doorstep. It is a tribute to the energy and tenacity
of ordinary people that so many of those schemes have
been abandoned.

Yes – it can be done! It's sometimes impossible to believe
that individuals can defeat the nuclear juggernaut as it
staggers relentlessly onwards. Three Mile Island,
Chernobyl and Sellafield are well-known nuclear names.
But other names should be better known. For instance,
not many people outside Cornwall have heard of
Luxulyan – but you should have!

Luxulyan used to be just another picturesque small
village, until the day that local people heard that a
drilling rig was being set up in a field outside the village
to test the suitability of the area for a nuclear power
station. A handful of people rushed up to the site and
without thinking parked a car in the gateway. They were
told there was nothing they could do. They refused to
move the car, and increased the blockade by digging
ditches at all exits to the field containing the drilling
rig. The Cornish flag flew proudly for several months.
The local police pointed out that they were on private
land (of a very sympathetic farmer) and that it was
therefore a civil matter.

The occupation was only ended by a High Court order;
the occupiers marched from the site at the head of over
1,000 local supporters, accompanied by music from the
local police band! It came as no surprise when the CEGB
announced that they were withdrawing plans for a
nuclear station anywhere in Cornwall. That's what
mobilizing the whole community is all about.

Other communities have been similarly successful.
Plans to dump high-level waste in North Wales were

withdrawn for a variety of reasons, not least because of the persistent obstruction of the surveyors by local people wherever they went. In Billingham, the whole community united to defeat plans to dump intermediate-level nuclear waste down a disused salt-mine.

You will find guidelines on how to run a campaign in the appendix at the back of this book, but in all these cases, urban or rural, people have won the day through using the same tactics. Firstly, make as much noise as possible as fast as possible. Let the local and national press know you're angry and determined. Secondly, stick to the point. This may come as a surprise in a book about protecting the environment, but if you are faced with a major local crisis, mobilize your community around *that* crisis. Don't expect people who've always believed nuclear power to be somehow 'necessary' to switch to outright opposition overnight. Remember, if they see you are right about this, then maybe they'll realize you are right about all those other environmental issues.

Energy is a crucial factor in all our lives. In Britain we use energy very inefficiently, particularly in the home. The results are high energy bills, dampness, disconnections for those who can't afford to pay, a waste of our precious fossil fuel resources and continuing damage to the environment. There are many different ways we can reduce this inefficiency and the impact of these problems. Some of these require persistent pressure on central government or on our local authorities. Others can be put into practice now, if we as individual consumers choose to do so.

RESOURCES

Books:

There are literally thousands of books on the issues in this section. For an up-to-date look at renewable energy, Friends of the Earth have produced *Energy*

Without End (FoE, 1986). Send an s.a.e. for FoE's Energy Resource List.

The best basic book on nuclear power remains *Nuclear Power* by Walt Patterson (Penguin, 1976).

The Energy Fix by Porter, Spence and Thompson (Pluto, 1986) takes a well-informed and detailed look at the politics of energy.

Organizations:

Friends of the Earth campaign for a safe energy policy and against nuclear power. There are 220 campaigning groups around Britain, and FoE now works in 31 countries around the world.

NATTA is the Network for Alternative Technology and Technology Assessment and produces a regular bulletin. Details from NATTA, Faculty of Technology, Open University, Walton Hall, Milton Keynes MK7 6AA.

Neighbourhood Energy Action runs many energy conservation schemes around Britain and can advise on setting up one in your area. Contact NEA, 2/4 Bigg Market, Newcastle-upon-Tyne.

Intermediate Technology Development Group (ITDG), 9 King St, London WC2E 8HN, produce a wide range of material on renewable energy supplies.

The Centre for Alternative Technology, Llwyngern Quarry, Machynlleth, Powys, Wales, has a permanent exhibition on renewable energy, organic gardening and many other aspects of improving your own environment. They are open for visits and also have a mail-order book service. Send s.a.e. for details.

SCRAM, 11 Forth St, Edinburgh, is a Scottish anti-nuclear organization that produces the bi-monthly SCRAM Energy Bulletin. It covers nuclear issues, but also gives excellent coverage to energy conservation and new energy supply systems.

8.
GETTING
THERE

Every day of our lives we make decisions about how we will move around during the next few hours. For the great majority of us these remain strictly individual choices, and we don't think very much about their relevance for others. We fail to realize the intimate connection between our patterns of movement and the quality of our surrounding environment.

However, sometimes we do notice the results. We can't get a seat on the bus, there's a traffic jam, the city seems even smellier, noisier and more unpleasant than usual. Occasionally we notice the opposite – our own road seems quiet, we decide to walk for a change, there seems no reason to worry about children being out on their bikes, our local town appears a pleasant, civilized sort of place to be.

Lots of us also think there is freedom of choice – that we can all pick and choose our own mode of transport, and that the government remains neutral in the background. Unfortunately, that was seldom the case in the past, and is now less true than ever. Governments intervene more and more in favour of some modes, such as private cars and heavy lorries, while other types of transport, trains, or the humble bicycle, find themselves out of favour.

Different choices – individual and collective – have greatly differing impacts on our environment. This is as true for the movement of goods as of people, and in a small, mostly urban country, the results of these decisions are greatly magnified. So can we transport ourselves about without doing too much harm to our environment? Can we move ourselves and our goods without excess noise, fumes and danger to ourselves and others?

CARS

The heart of the problem, undoubtedly, is the private car. Either moving or stationary, its use of space is highly inefficient, and there are particular problems about it in city centres, in residential streets, and for journeys to work. The benefits people derive from their cars are often outweighed by collective disadvantages. Increasingly, local authorities feel obliged to impose controls on the car in order to allow local people to retain some freedom of movement.

Road safety:
Although overall casualty figures have fallen in recent years, those for cyclists and certain classes of pedestrians have risen. So the first thing to say is – slow down! No one is as good a driver as they think they are, and most

people are hopeless judges both of their reaction times and of stopping distances. Better still, take an advanced driving course, if only to improve your insurance rating.

Never, ever, drive when you have been drinking alcohol. Many people are dangerous well below the legal limit. Fortunately a tide of legislation around the world is rapidly rubbing drink-driving off the map. In Australia, the introduction of random breath-testing reduced drink accidents by a third. In the US, Mothers Against Drinking and Driving (MADD) have forced state after state to pass measures like banning open drinks in cars and setting up road blocks to catch drink-drivers. This tide has hit Europe with random breath-testing and reductions in the legal limit in Scandinavia and Finland, and a massive new police drive in France.

Pressure in Britain is mounting with the formation of CADD, the Campaign Against Drinking and Driving, all of whose members are people who have lost a relative through a drinking driver. They recommend simple remedies that anyone can take. Travel by public transport or taxi. Don't give or buy drinks for people you know are driving. Always provide interesting alternatives to alcohol when serving drinks at parties.

Extend these notions of care into your everyday driving. A moment's impatience in a car may cause a lifetime of regret. In the past, careless and dangerous driving has been very lightly punished. Now our laws and sentencing are being updated, and antisocial conduct is much more likely to get the severe punishment it deserves.

More people have lost their lives in road accidents since 1945 than were killed on active service in World War Two. Think of that next time you turn on the ignition!

The vehicle:
The average lifespan of British cars has declined dramatically in recent years, whereas in other countries it has improved. Check carefully for rust and general wear when buying a secondhand car. Consider whether life

would not be simpler and cheaper by using other forms
of transport most of the year, and just hiring a decent
car for the half-dozen times in a year you really need
it.

Fuel efficiency:

It is stating the obvious to say that smaller engines tend
to be more fuel-efficient. Even so, consumption can vary
wildly even for the same make of car. Constant stopping
and starting in traffic jams can produce some terrible
results – hardly surprising, considering that in places
like central London, the average speed of vehicles is only
11.5 mph/18.4 kph.

The Department of Transport publishes a useful leaflet
on ways to get more for your money, including simple
matters like taking junk out of the boot and taking off
unnecessary roof-racks. Other studies have shown that
the difference between 'aggressive' and 'normal' driving
can be as much as 20% of fuel consumption. And for most
cars, fuel efficiency starts to fall rapidly above 55 mph,
which was why this figure was set as the maximum speed
limit in the USA after the 1973 oil crisis.

Company cars:

Many people in middle and upper management have their
car or petrol, or both, provided by their firms, who can
then offset this expense against tax. While this may be
a cosy situation for all concerned, it actually amounts
to a scandalous subsidy to an already favoured element
of our society.

It also totally distorts our overall transport system –
in 1984 company car subsidies amounted to £2 billion,
more money than the combined subsidy for all our
railways and buses. This artificial stimulus to commuting
traffic causes havoc, especially in the urban rush hour,
as people are paid to use cars unnecessarily and offload
all the disadvantages onto society at large.

Noise:

We all have to put up with a lot of noise. It is now possible to reduce vehicle noise at source, but this isn't much use if we allow traffic volumes to keep rising. Getting a decrease in the volume of traffic in your street is the best way of tackling the problem.

Excess motorcycle noise can be dealt with by local traffic police. Ask your local council about how to complain about noise from lorry operators' yards. Lorry noise at night is a good reason for seeking a night-time ban. Aircraft noise is a complex issue; take it up with your MP in the first instance.

Lastly, if you are unfortunate enough to suffer increased traffic noise as a result of living on a new or 'improved' road, you may be entitled to a noise insulation grant. There is a Department of the Environment leaflet explaining this – ask your council for a copy.

PUBLIC TRANSPORT

Problems about pollution, congestion, road safety and unequal access to cars all underline the need for reliable and cheap public transport. If this can be made efficient and popular enough, as in many European cities, it often proves enough of a carrot to get drivers out of their cars of their own accord. (The stick of controls can be quietly put away.) Alas, in Britain the impression is all too often given that high levels of car ownership and a thriving public transport system cannot co-exist. In fact this is quite untrue, as nations such as Germany and Holland show.

Rail:

The fact is that rail – which includes railways, light rail, metro and underground – is the only sensible way of moving large numbers of people in and out of cities with minimal impact. Mainland European cities have accepted this for decades. The USA, which once favoured the automobile-based city, is rapidly changing its mind, with multi-billion dollar public investment in local rail systems. Some of these are even being constructed by removing a lane from a nearby motorway!

This contrasts dramatically with Britain, where the government is cutting funds for British Rail by one-third over a four-year period. The result: breakdowns, unreliability, semi-derelict unstaffed stations, and overcrowding.

If you have a complaint about rail travel, start with your station manager. From them you can get the address of BR's Area Manager, and also of the local Transport Users' Consultative Committee, which is the statutory body set up to handle passengers' problems. A letter to the chairman of BR (Sir Robert Reid, B.R.B., 22 Marylebone Road, London NW1 6JJ) won't go amiss either. Large numbers of lines, particularly in rural areas, have some form of support group these days, which are banded together under the umbrella of the Railway Development Society. And at a national level, TRANSPORT 2000 provides an authoritative voice on rail matters.

Buses:
There is no doubt that the bus is the Cinderella of our transport system. Bus passengers usually get the worst treatment of all in terms of availability, conditions, fares and information. But for overwhelming numbers of young people, the elderly and women, the bus service is a lifeline, not just to school and the shops but to hospitals, libraries, leisure facilities, the social services, and for keeping in touch with friends and relatives.

Friends of the Earth did a study of bus cuts in four rural areas in 1984, and discovered many people whose horizons had shrunk dramatically because of bus cuts. Conversely, when the Greater London Council changed to a cheaper, better service in the 1980s, people who had felt like prisoners in their own homes came out to travel much more freely.

But the GLC's policies produced other results. Firstly, when travellers are tempted on to public transport, road accidents fall markedly. Secondly, that it is possible to

get people to change their patterns of travel simply by offering a better service. At the end of 1984, by comparison with 1982, bus use in London had risen by 13% and tube use by 44%. Car commuting had fallen by 21%.

However, the abolition of the big urban authorities and the effects of the 1985 Transport Act have changed all this; it looks as if the old downward spiral of decline will continue. The full consequences of the Act, to deregulate services and to reduce subsidies, will not be known for some time, but they are unlikely to lead to the creation of many extra services.

Because bus users have no statutory body to protect them, Bus Users' Groups have sprung up in different parts of the country, and TRANSPORT 2000 is operating a monitoring scheme called 'Buswatch'. Joining this provides an excellent way of getting involved in the fight to retain services.

CYCLISTS AND PEDESTRIANS

74% of all recorded journeys are of 8 km or less. Many of these are on foot or cycle – and many more would be if conditions were made more pleasant. Whereas a mere 4% of all journeys travelled in this country are by bike, in Denmark the figure often approaches 40%.

The highly traditional engineering professions in Britain have done little since the war to help the cyclist and pedestrian – building rural motorways and urban clearways is obviously more prestigious. Cyclists have been ignored in most new road schemes. Pedestrians have to tackle mountainous footbridges and forbidding subways. And if you have any disability – hard luck!

But it is precisely these neglected areas that offer the greatest opportunity for personal effort and practical action. Start by reclaiming your own street! If it suffers from illegal parking, ask your local authority to see that traffic wardens deal with the matter. If it suffers from speeding traffic, ask the local police to tackle it. If it is a primarily residential street, consider ways of reducing vehicle speeds. At long last, road humps – common on the Continent – are to be allowed here. See if they are appropriate to your road. Broken paving, potholes in the road, out-of-action street lights, broken glass in the gutters – on all of these you can prod the local council into action.

Local councils are sometimes reluctant to put in pedestrian crossings because of highly detailed standards to which they must conform. But islands or 'refuges' in the middle of the road are simpler, cheaper, and often more effective.

Did you know that councils can vary the 'response time' and 'green person phase' at signalled crossings? Do some timings with your watch, and complain if you think the times inadequate. Study how long it takes pensioners to cross in safety.

Cyclists suffer particularly badly from bad road surfaces and poor facilities. Features common throughout most of Europe – cycle phases at junctions, special cycle crossings, purpose-built routes, exemption from car control measures – are almost entirely absent from this country. There is bound to be some form of cycle campaign group in your area, and contacting them is the first step towards getting things put right.

Some cycle groups may be working on specific projects, such as building routes on derelict land (e.g. disused railway lines), campaigning for BMX facilities for youngsters, or doing a 'Safe routes to school' study. Many cycle and pedestrian schemes can be incorporated as part of General Improvement Areas, where local councils are upgrading rundown parts of town.

WOMEN

Many of the issues we have discussed so far have particular implications for women. As 70% of adult women do not drive at all, and only a minority of the remainder have first call on the 'family' car, they are far more likely to be interested in the quality of public transport, especially buses. Neglected questions such as halting the destaffing on railway stations and buses should come much more to the fore. The design of subways, buildings and transport interchanges to enhance feelings of personal security is an issue crying out for attention.

A number of local councils now have Women's Committees, and you could ask these to take an interest in such questions. Friends of the Earth have produced a pioneering booklet on the issue, and have just set up their 'Women and Transport' campaign.

LORRIES

Heavy lorries are an out-and-out menace. The British government's decision in 1983 to allow the weight of fully-laden lorries to go up from 32½ to 38 tonnes has meant more broken bridges and smashed road surfaces, and considerable damage to underground services such as water, gas and sewers.

In 1986, the GLC imposed a London-wide ban on unnecessary lorry traffic at night and during weekends.

Essential transport was exempt from the ban. Similar bans could be imposed in other cities – especially if residents demand them. Elsewhere there is a wide variety of weight and width restrictions that can already be legally enforced, particularly on heavier lorries.

Particular difficulties can arise over lorries carrying sand, gravel and coal, especially from open-cast workings. Here the secret is to spot potential problems from new developments when they are first proposed. If at all possible, see to it that planning permission is only granted if some or all of the loads travel by rail.

Getting lorries out of towns is often put forward as a reason for allowing new developments in the countryside, even in Green Belt areas. Beware of this argument: a little peace may indeed be achieved, but only at the cost of losing open land, allowing further urban sprawl, promoting further traffic congestion and adding to the flow of jobs away from town centres. So keep an eye on the local press for details of any new development – and ask who's really going to benefit from it.

RESOURCES

Contacts:

As you may have gathered, your local council has a great deal to do with transport matters. Although they have little real power, parish councils are a good forum for airing all kinds of matters. District councils also have relatively limited powers, but often act as the agents of the county council in England and Wales (regions in Scotland) in matters such as new roads, cycle and pedestrian affairs and road safety. Counties have a lot of flexibility over whether they want to support bus and train services. The London boroughs have in theory had a great deal of freedom since the end of the GLC; in practice, they have found themselves severely circumscribed by central government.

All counties have to have structure plans, outlining what is and is not permissible development. Examining these (there will be copies at Town Halls and reference libraries) gives an invaluable insight into what's going on. They can be used as arguments should you wish to oppose any development you feel undesirable. District councils also have local plans for the whole district.

The Department of Transport (2 Marsham Street, London SW1P 3EB) is the ultimate authority and guardian of the purse-strings. It has come under severe criticism from environmentalists in recent years for being dominated by the 'roads lobby'. Transport letters should always be copied to the Secretary of State for Transport.

For an alternative voice, try TRANSPORT 2000 (10 Melton Street, London NW1). This is a coalition of all the main bodies concerned with transport and environmental matters. T2000 has an excellent magazine, *Transport Report*, and are also the coordinators of Buswatch.

Among T2000's members are The Civic Trust (17 Carlton House Terrace, London SW1), and the Council for the Protection of Rural England (4 Hobart Place, London SW1).

For **rail**, it is worth contacting the Secretary of the Railway Development Society (15 Clapham Road, Lowestoft, Suffolk).

For active **cyclists**, Friends of the Earth have run a campaign for over 10 years. They produce a wealth of information and service the groups of the Cycle Campaign Network. Despite its name, the Cyclists' Touring Club (69 Meadrow, Godalming, Surrey) also campaigns vigorously for the rights of everyday cyclists. It also offers advice on legal, touring and equipment matters.

For **pedestrians**, the Pedestrians' Association (1–5 Wandsworth Road, London SW8) is worth belonging to because of its excellent magazine, *Walk*. The Ramblers Association is at the same address. The address of the Campaign Against Drink Driving is c/o John Knight, Meadside, Shudy Camps, Cambridge CB1 6RA. The National Consumer Council (18 Queen Anne's Gate, London SW1 9AA) has come up with a self-help pack for improving your local pedestrian environment. They are also increasingly interested in the quality of bus and rail services.

People interested in the welfare of those with **disabilities** should contact the Joint Committees of the Blind and Partially Sighted, (224 Portland Street, London W1N 6AA), and the Disabled (9 Moss Close, Pinner, Middlesex HA5 3AY).

All of the above organizations will have plenty of further literature to recommend, but a few ideas to follow up are given below.

Publications:
For a shorter version of what needs to be done, see FoE's Transport Policy, *Getting There* (1986).

Friends of the Earth have also produced an information pack called *Cities for People*. Although based on problems in London, its illustration of the way all issues interrelate in urban areas is applicable to all towns and cities. For further information on heavy lorries, see FoE's Transport Paper, Number 3.

The road safety scandal is graphically highlighted in *Danger on the Road: The Needless Scourge* by Hillman Plowden (Policy Studies Institute, 1984). Stephen Plowden's *Taming Traffic* (André Deutsch, 1980) remains an excellent overview of the transport scene in the UK.

The most helpful and inspiring book about cycling is still *Richard's Bicycle Book* by Richard Ballantine, published by Pan. And all drivers and cyclists ought to read FoE's *Guide to Cycle Friendly Motoring*.

9.
THE
POLLUTION
SOLUTION

Pollution is a catch-all word for some of the most serious environmental problems we face today. The very fabric of our natural ecosystems is being corroded by a variety of toxic inputs; species face extinction, whole forests are dying, lakes and rivers can no longer support life, soils are poisoned, and even the seas are now threatened.

The problem of pollution has faced humans since the first time we began to change natural cycles by using tools to dig metals from the ground. In prehistoric times, this process was local; but as populations grew and human inventiveness with it, the problems became greater. The natural cycles of many elements, like lead, sulphur and nitrogen, have all been radically altered by human industrial and domestic activities. Sulphur, for instance, is naturally put into the atmosphere as sulphur dioxide from volcanic explosions, and some air/sea exchange at the oceans' surface. But now, in the northern hemisphere, more than 90% of sulphur dioxide in the atmosphere comes from artificial sources, chiefly the burning of fossil fuels like coal and oil in power stations.

The readiness of humankind to use the Earth's resources for its own good without any care for the safe disposal of waste products has led to an appalling decline in the ability of the planet to sustain life. Pollution is a problem that affects us all. If the air that we breathe is foul, and the seas that we swim in are a health hazard, then individual action on its own is bound to be limited.

If we want our children to inherit clean air, water and soil, we must take collective responsibility for not fouling the nest.

VEHICLE EXHAUSTS

Useful as cars undoubtedly are, they are becoming one of the greatest threats to Europe's forests, and to human health. The fumes that come from car exhausts (largely invisible except on a cold morning) contain a number of chemicals that can wreak havoc upon the environment.

The first and foremost of these is lead, which is added to petrol by oil companies as an anti-knock agent. It has been known for many years that lead is toxic to humans, and in particular to children. The major source of environmental lead, by far, is petrol exhausts, yet we still drive around in this country with leaded petrol, long after many other countries like the US and Japan have banned it.

Lead can cause hyperactivity and loss of learning ability in young children; it can even cross the placental blood barrier in mothers and cause brain damage to unborn babies. It wasn't until the summer of 1986 that a few petrol stations in and around London began to stock unleaded petrol, and this despite years of hard campaigning from action groups like CLEAR (Campaign for Lead Free Air) and CALIP (the Campaign Against Lead in Petrol).

In West Germany, it is hoped that more than 50% of all cars will be using lead-free petrol by the end of 1986. We're a long way off such a target in the UK, and yet it could be achieved if there was the will to do so from the oil companies and the government. If you drive a car, ask your local garage if they're intending to stock unleaded petrol — and keep asking until they do!

The other chemicals that are continuously pumped out of the exhaust pipes of cars and lorries are carbon monoxide, nitrogen oxides (NOx) and hydrocarbons. Carbon monoxide can be a hazard in confined spaces and in heavy traffic congestion, but the other two components are of more immediate concern.

Nitrogen oxide on its own can be converted to nitric acid in the atmosphere, and is one of the two major components (the other being sulphur dioxide) of acid rain. When deposited as rain, mist or even dust, nitrogen oxide contributes to the acidification of the environment. In lakes, this can mean turning the water as acid as vinegar, to the obvious detriment of fish and all other life. 57 lakes in Scotland are already losing their fish because of acidification, and in Canada, Sweden and Norway, the number of dead lakes runs into tens of thousands.

Moreover, in combination with hydrocarbons, nitrogen oxide can form yet another harmful gas – ozone. While ozone is a necessary gas in the *outer* layers of the atmosphere, to protect the earth from ultraviolet rays, it is poisonous to crops and trees down at ground level. The West Germans, who have already seen more than half of their forests damaged by air pollution, are convinced that ozone, in combination with acid rain, is responsible for 'Waldsterben', or forest die-back. In some areas of Germany, such as the Black Forest, more than 80% of the trees are dead or dying. The death of the forests could be the greatest single environmental tragedy to confront Europe this century. Environmentalists are campaigning for speed limits of 100 kph to be brought in. This is quite simply because the faster cars go, the more the pollutants spew from their exhausts.

Apart from driving more slowly, and turning off the engine to conserve fuel in traffic jams or when stopped at traffic lights, there are technological solutions to some of the air pollution problems caused by cars. One approach, favoured both by our government and by British manufacturers, is to develop 'lean-burn engines'. These use petrol more efficiently and considerably reduce carbon monoxide and nitrogen oxide.

But, unfortunately, lean-burn engines do little to prevent the emission of hydrocarbons, and that is critical, not only because they contribute to ozone formation, but because they pose a health hazard themselves. Benz-a-pyrene (the carcinogenic agent in cigarette smoke) is just one of the hydrocarbons that make vehicle exhaust fumes so dangerous.

It is likely that some 2,000–3,000 urban lung cancer deaths every year in England and Wales come about as a direct result of the regular inhalation of vehicle exhausts. To reduce hydrocarbons, three-way catalytic converters can be fitted to car exhausts. The only problem with these is that they are 'poisoned' by lead in petrol, and so can only be used if unleaded petrol is widely available.

It is quite untrue, as many opponents of catalysts have claimed, that fuel efficiency and performance are significantly reduced by their use. Likewise, the argument that catalysts are too expensive is a myth, and in some countries, firms like Fiat and Volvo are offering free catalyzer systems with new cars, as they realize that this is now an attractive selling point to an environmentally-conscious public.

If you are considering buying a car, then look into the possibility of buying one with the most up-to-date technology available in this country. If you want to buy

British, but find that only the foreign manufacturers are really bothered about this issue, then write to the manufacturer and tell them why they have lost your custom. Display a sticker on your car saying you use lead-free petrol, or that you don't drive over 100 km per hour (both available from FoE).

And don't rush to change to diesel, thinking it's a more environmentally acceptable fuel – the hydrocarbon emissions from diesel are even more of a health hazard than those from ordinary petrol.

POWER STATIONS

Sulphur dioxide (SO_2), emitted from coal- and oil-fired power stations, is the single most important contributor to acid rain. It is implicated in the corrosion of historic monuments like St Paul's Cathedral in London, the decline of birds like the dipper, losses in crop yields, extinction of fish populations, threats to human health (by increasing the rate at which heavy metals leach into groundwater supplies) and the decline in vitality of tree species like beech, yew and Scots pine. To stop acid rain, we must first clean up our existing power stations, and then make sure that new ones are fitted with more efficient technologies. Ultimately, we must look towards energy conservation and renewable energy sources to reduce pollution.

Coal- and oil-fired power stations were already being fitted with tall chimney stacks in the 1960s. All this did, however, was to allow the transport of gases like sulphur dioxide and nitrogen oxide many hundreds of miles away, often to another country. What goes up must come down – and Britain is not known as the 'Dirty Man of Europe' for nothing!

We are in fact the largest emitter of sulphur dioxide in Western Europe. Current figures for annual emissions are around 3.8 million tonnes, and much of that goes over the North Sea to Norway, Sweden, Holland and Belgium. Norway receives more sulphur pollution from Britain than it puts out from its own power stations. The Central Electricity Generating Board now accounts for more than 70% of Britain's sulphur emissions, and has done little to reduce its contribution to the problem. In September 1986 the British government announced that the CEGB would be fitting desulphurization equipment to just three power stations. However, to achieve a 60% reduction in sulphur dioxide output by 1995, which is the minimum target we should be aiming for, would mean fitting desulphurization equipment to twelve power stations, at a cost to the average consumer of perhaps an extra £2 or £3 a year. Write to the CEGB and tell them you are willing to pay this minuscule amount to get them to clean up their act.

THE GREENHOUSE EFFECT

The 'greenhouse effect' is what happens when carbon dioxide (CO_2) builds up in the atmosphere, limiting the amount of heat that can escape. Carbon dioxide levels have risen enormously over the last fifty years and, if this continues, it will eventually mean a global warming of perhaps 1° or 2°C. The smallest global warming could be catastrophic, leading to a partial melting of the polar ice caps and hence a rise in sea-levels. Vast areas of currently isolated land, including many major cities, would be submerged.

There is no way to eliminate the emission of carbon dioxide from the combustion process, so the only answer to the problem is to reduce the amount of combustion, in other words to use less energy. It would also help if we stopped destroying the world's forests. Trees use up carbon dioxide in their respiration process, and thus have an important role to play in maintaining current levels.

THE OZONE LAYER

Though ozone is very damaging at ground level, it plays

a critical role in maintaining life on earth. A band of ozone
in the upper atmosphere helps protect us from ultraviolet
(UV) radiation. The ozone filters out the most harmful
rays. Skin cancer is already at virtually epidemic levels
in Northern Europe, as people expose themselves to
abnormally high ultraviolet levels by sunbathing at every
opportunity. If the ozone layer is depleted, then the
ultraviolet reaching us here on earth will be increasingly
dangerous.

Once again, it is the activities of humans that are
causing the problems. The ozone layer has remained
intact for thousands of years, but scientists have now
found a huge hole in the layer, directly above the
Antarctic ice cap. It is not yet known how the hole was
caused, but it *is* known that the propellants from aerosol
cans and the fluids used in refrigeration processes
contribute to the depletion of ozone in the atmosphere.

Just take a look around your own home and take note
of all the aerosol cans you use. How many are really
necessary? If you do need to spray something, then there
are several types of air-propellant containers available
that depend just on natural sources. If in doubt, then
contact the National Society for Clean Air, who will be
able to provide information on the effects of propellants
on the atmosphere, and on many other related
problems.

MARINE POLLUTION

The constantly moving surface of the sea, and the regular,
predictable changing of the tides, conceals a major
disaster in the making. The seas underpin crucial
chemical cycles, like those of sulphur and sodium; they
are the source of the greatest amount of biomass on the
planet; they provide protein in vast quantities in the form
of fish; and they have a profound effect on rainfall and
weather patterns. To use them as a rubbish dump for
our effluent is a policy of the most staggering
shortsightedness.

The problems of pollution in the sea are many, from the build-up of plastic rubbish, to the accumulation of radioactive waste in sediments. Along the way, there are pesticides, detergents, fertilizers, industrial effluents, harbour dredgings, oil spillages, human sewage, chemical wastes, heavy metals and ships' garbage. All of these things combine to make a toxic cocktail the oceans cannot resist. In Britain, organizations like Greenpeace, the Marine Conservation Society and the World Wildlife Fund are working to promote awareness of these problems. They have joined with Friends of the Earth to form the North Sea Working Group UK.

Some marine problems are highly visible, such as the discharge of untreated sewage into the sea. A swim off many of our most popular beaches is not only unsightly, but can now pose a real health hazard.

An EEC Directive on bathing beaches was supposed to have done something to alleviate the problem, but Britain has been remarkably lax in its interpretation of the legislation. Countries were asked to notify the EEC of 'beaches that are used by large numbers of bathers'. Britain decided that 'large numbers' meant a threshold of 1,500 bathers per mile of beach, or 500 swimmers in the water at the same time. This ridiculous classification method meant that out of more than 600 beaches in

England and Wales, only 27 are classified as bathing beaches! Both France and Italy notified 3,000 beaches, and even Luxembourg, which has no coastline at all, put forward more than Britain, with 39 beaches!

Incredibly, even out of Britain's 27 designated beaches, 6 still fail to comply with the EEC bacteriological standards, and 3 have had to be granted exemptions from water quality regulations. The state of Britain's beaches can be seen more accurately in the *Golden Guide*, published by the Coastal Anti-Pollution League.

If you believe there is a problem with the sea in your area, then get the local council to test for bacteriological contamination, and ask these questions of your water authority:

- is it aware of the EEC requirements to reduce the amount of sewage sludge pumped into the sea?
- does it intend to monitor or control industrial effluent at each of its sea outfalls?
- can it tell you the time taken for sewage to come ashore again after being pumped out?
- will it give you access to the results of basic investigations necessary to assess the efficiency of the outfall?

OIL POLLUTION

Although it has dropped from the headlines in recent years, oil pollution is still a major hazard for seabirds, and an amenity problem on many beaches. Particularly in the northern part of the North Sea, oil pollution incidents are on the increase.

While one individual cannot do much to stop the illegal discharge of waste oil at sea, or prevent shipping accidents, you can report any sightings of birds that are killed by oil. So, walking along a beach, keep an eye open for oiled birds, count them, try and identify the species and report all finds to the Royal Society for the Protection of Birds (RSPB) or the British Trust for Ornithology (BTO). Also look to see if they have small metal rings on their legs. If they do, then take the ring off and send it to the British Museum of Natural History. The bird ringing scheme is run by the BTO, and can yield very valuable information about the place of origin of the birds and often about the origin of the oil.

Along the shore also watch out for oil drums, packages marked 'hazard', fishing nets and packing cases. The Advisory Committee on Pollution of the Sea keeps a register of sightings of all these items and would value information on their whereabouts. If anything you find is marked with a hazard sign or radioactive sign (yes, those containers have been lost at sea as well!), then don't mess about – contact your local coastguard or police station immediately.

DETERGENTS AND EUTROPHICATION

Until recently it took a long time for detergents to stop working. They remained active in drains, sewers and rivers – the most tell-tale sign of them being the slabs of foam (or 'foambergs') often seen below weirs. Although modern detergents no longer cause this particular problem, they're still an environmental menace.

Many of our rivers and lakes are naturally short of plant nutrients. But extra nutrients get into the water from farmland and from sewage works. These extra nutrients stimulate the growth of minute plants, so that once clear water soon looks like pea soup. Other water plants then die off because they're cast into the shade, which in turn means less food and shelter for fish, and less food for waterfowl and other birds. This destructive process is called 'eutrophication'.

The process depends upon an excess of both nitrates and phosphates. Most of the nitrates come from farmland. This means that the only way significantly to reduce the amount entering our rivers is to reduce the use of fertilizers.

It would be easier, at least in the short term, to reduce the amounts of phosphate. Because most phosphate enters rivers from sewage works, it can be controlled by fitting special equipment at the sewage works to clean up the effluent before it enters the river. This simple and relatively cheap process is called 'phosphate stripping'. But only a very few sewage works have installed the relevant equipment.

Virtually all the detergents used in this country are based on phosphate, and nearly half the phosphate in sewage effluent comes from detergents. This means that one household switching to detergents which do not contain phosphate only makes a small difference, because large amounts of phosphate will continue to enter the sewers from households still using phosphate-based detergents. Phosphate-free detergents such as Ecover are not widely available, and are still more expensive, but it's worthwhile trying to get hold of them. Even this small gesture makes a difference.

DRINKING WATER

As well as contributing to eutrophication, nitrates also pollute the water supplies of millions of people in Britain. As agriculture is the main source of this pollution, it is not surprising that the problem is most serious in the most intensively farmed regions.

The possible link between nitrates and cancer of the stomach and the gut remains the subject of considerable debate. The British government originally accepted the World Health Organization's (WHO) recommendations about safe levels for nitrates in drinking water. Indeed, it subsequently justified its decision to grant exemptions for those water sources which contained nitrate levels above the more stringent maximum level specified in the EEC's Drinking Water Directive on the grounds that the EEC should have adopted the WHO standards. But when the WHO subsequently decided to recommend even more stringent levels than those set by the EEC, the government suddenly discovered that it didn't have much faith in the WHO either!

Many of the drinking water sources with high levels of nitrates also contain high levels of agro-chemicals. This problem is most serious in eastern England, where a number of sources contain levels of herbicide well above the limits set in the EEC Directive.

SILAGE AND SLURRY

Slurry and the run-off from silage are two farm products which cause serious water pollution. This relatively new problem is largely a result of the recent trend towards large-scale dairy and pig farming.

Large dairy herds need massive quantities of silage (specially treated grass) as winter feed. But when fresh grass is converted into silage, it releases large amounts of a very smelly liquid. Though this run-off is a potentially valuable animal food, it is often wasted because it leaks from the silage pit.

Slurry has also become more of a problem as dairy herds have got bigger, and slats have replaced straw bedding in cattle sheds. Though some farmers still spray slurry on to fields, more and more of them rely on artificial fertilizers. This means that large amounts of slurry are often stored as waste in tanks near to cattle sheds.

Both silage pits and slurry tanks are often located far too close to streams or ditches. Any leaks inevitably end up causing serious water pollution. Some farmers even allow excess silage run-off or slurry to drain into nearby streams. Such pollution is a criminal offence under the 1974 Control of Pollution Act, but the number of farmers who get caught is minimal, and the amount they are fined is paltry.

HAZARDOUS WASTE

Recent reports from the Department of the Environment's Hazardous Waste Inspectorate have revealed that the management of toxic wastes in Britain is in a dire state.

While some companies are taking care to abide by the laws and regulations, others are undercutting their prices by disregarding safety practices. Asbestos is often buried at too shallow a depth and without workers wearing protective clothing; drums of toxic wastes are left in piles (they are not supposed to touch) in tips where water collects and corrodes the metal; liquid toxic chemicals are in danger of leaching through the soil of the tips into drinking water supplies. Worst of all is the practice of dumping poisonous chemical wastes in unlicensed (and therefore uncontrolled) sites.

If you see piles of chemical drums lying at a site in your area, then inform the Hazardous Waste Inspectorate immediately. Likewise, if you see anyone dumping at night, or if there are large gaps in the fences around tips. As to your own wastes, don't throw anything into your rubbish bin that is toxic, as it will not be noticed by refuse authorities and will just be taken to an ordinary domestic tip.

If you have materials like old pesticides, slug pellets, medicines, cleaning fluids or building materials like creosote, then contact your local Waste Disposal Authority about where to take them. Remember that car sump oil should be disposed of (or preferably recycled) in special containers, and never burned or poured down the street drains. And don't burn rubber, plastics or old furniture – toxic fumes are given off in large quantities. Always take this material to a tip, or have your local authority pick it up.

A DIRTY BUSINESS

Pollution poses a serious problem for all of us. The government may pay lip-service to the 'Polluter Pays' principle, but you can be sure that this is the exception rather than the rule. Polluters, be they individuals or businesses, are as dirty as the pollution they cause. To feather their own nest, they foul everyone else's – and they'll go on doing it until they're forced to stop.

RESOURCES

Books:
Mary Lean, *Pollution and the Environment*
(Macdonald, 1985)
Steve Elsworth, *Acid Rain*
(Pluto Press, 1985)
Adam Markham and Chris Rose (editors), *Acid Rain – Yesterday, Today, Tomorrow*
(FoE, 1986)
Des Wilson, *The Lead Scandal*
(Heinemann, 1983)
Rachel Carson, *Silent Spring*
(Penguin, 1965)
World Resources Institute/International Institute for Environment and Development, *World Resources 1986*
(Basic Books, 1986)

Magazines:
Ambio – A journal of the Human Environment
Pergamon Press

New Scientist
   IPC Magazines
Acid News
   The Swedish NGO Secretariat on Acid Rain
AIRPLAN Bulletin
   Air Pollution Action Network/FoE International
North Sea Monitor
   Werkgroep Noordzee
These last three magazines can all be obtained from
Friends of the Earth.

Organizations:
CLEAR (Campaign for Lead Free Air), 3 Endsleigh St,
   London WC1 0DD.
CALIP (Campaign Against Lead in Petrol), 171 Barnett
   Wood Lane, Ashtead, Surrey KT21 2LP.
NSCA (National Society for Clean Air), 136 North Street,
   Brighton, East Sussex BN1 1RG.
Greenpeace, 36 Graham Street, London N1.
Marine Conservation Society, 4 Gloucester Rd, Ross-on-
   Wye, Herefordshire.
ACOPS (Advisory Committee on Pollution of the Sea),
   3 Endsleigh Street, London WC1H 0DD.
British Trust for Ornithology, Beech Grove, Tring,
   Herts.
Royal Society for the Protection of Birds, The Lodge,
   Sandy, Bedfordshire.
North Sea Working Group (UK), c/o Friends of the Earth,
   377 City Road, London EC1V 1NA.
World Wildlife Fund, Panda House, 11–13 Ockford Rd,
   Godalming, Surrey GU7 1QU.

10.
USING THE LAND

We all need to 'get away from it all', to find some quiet place which helps to soothe away the stresses of everyday living. Why else are weekend visits to the countryside, fishing trips and the like so popular? And surely most of us remember the particular joy we experienced in the 'secret places' of our childhood. It's a fair bet that those places were relatively wild places.

For those of us who live on the edge of urban areas or near large parks, this relaxation can be found on our doorstep. For others it's not so easy. Too many of us live in grim surroundings. We are penned in by buildings, polluted by car and lorry exhausts, and when out and

about we need to be on constant alert to avoid being run over. The countryside is so far away it might as well be on another planet. The only nearby 'green bits' are boring stretches of grass dotted with the odd tree – the grass is often a 'no go area' for children and the trees are too small for climbing.

But almost *all* of us take the quality of our surroundings for granted. It's only when a cherished area is destroyed by building development, a new road, waste tipping or by modern farming techniques, that we feel directly affected. Is development more important than anything else? Could we have influenced events while the development was still at the planning stage? How can we take practical action to improve the quality of our surroundings? What are wildlife gardens, ecological parks and city farms?

YOUR NATURAL HERITAGE

Sadly, many attempts to prevent the destruction of wildlife habitats in urban areas fail for one simple reason. They are too late. They only start when the damage has begun – when someone sees the bulldozers going into action.

The key to success is getting early warning of proposed developments. This requires knowing where to find out what is planned and when.

Your district council is responsible for day-to-day planning matters. The planning policies for the area are laid down in local plans. The local plan sets the scene for development. Any proposals which are out of step with the plan are unlikely to obtain planning permission. But even if the plan indicates that the area which you want to protect is *not* suitable for development, there is nothing to stop someone applying for planning permission.

And that's where you come in. It's up to you to keep an eye on things. All applications for planning permission have to be advertised in your local paper, and they're usually in some well-established weekly. Get used to buying that paper and checking out the 'planning permissions' adverts – usually well-hidden in among the classifieds. Most of them will be for 'illuminated signs' for hotels or a new shop front on the High Street, but occasionally you'll see an application for something like 'Warehousing to be built on open land to the rear of Redland Housing Estate'. It's only when you read that, and realize that 'open land' is a meadow full of wild flowers every spring, that you know you need to act.

Let us now assume that someone has applied for planning permission to develop the site. Your first step is formally to object to the application within three weeks of the date of the advertisement. This buys time. A brief formal letter saying that you object to planning application number 123 is all that is needed immediately. Then start to do your research. Making sure you know your facts is crucial.

Find out whether the land is shown on the district plan as suitable for the proposed development. If not, it is unlikely that the district council will grant permission. The county council may also decide to object if the proposed development conflicts with its own structure plan. This plan includes detailed conservation policies which may favour your case.

Even if these plans do not favour your case, do not give up. Find additional ways to oppose the proposed development. For instance, will the proposed development cause any traffic hazards? If so, the county council may object on 'highways grounds'.

Your objection to the proposed development will be strengthened if you can show that the site is a valuable habitat for wildlife. If it is particularly important, it may be one of Britain's 4,500 Sites of Special Scientific Interest (SSSI). These are designated by the Nature Conservancy Council, an official body. Even if the site is important enough to be an SSSI, it may not yet have been designated as one because of bureaucratic delays.

If the site is not an SSSI, it may still be a valuable refuge for wildlife. Contact your County Naturalists' Trust or museum, of which may have useful records of the wildlife in your area. They will also be able to assess the relative importance for wildlife of the site which you are trying to protect from development, and can be powerful allies.

If there are mature trees on the site, they may be protected by Tree Preservation Orders (TPOs). These are issued by district councils and details are held in a register which is open for inspection at the council's offices. As a TPO makes it illegal to cut down the trees in question, it must be cancelled before the trees can be removed for development to take place. By objecting to this, you can effectively obstruct the proposed development. If the development does eventually go ahead, your objections may result in some or all of the trees being retained, even if that involves a restriction upon the nature and extent of the development.

Gathering support:
As well as doing background research, it is also important to contact other people who want to see the site protected. Why not get together with a few friends and produce a leaflet which explains why the site is important as a local amenity, as a haven for wildlife, as an informal

playground for children, etc. Use the leaflet also to draw
attention to the threat, and perhaps to advertise a
meeting to set up a local action group (See Appendix page
150 for some ideas). Such meetings are a good place to get
your local councillors on your side, so make sure that
they are invited well beforehand since they are very busy
people.

Remember that it is those councillors who will make
the first decisions about the planning applications.

The fate of planning applications:
If your district council seems likely to grant permission
for the development – your local councillors should be
able to find out for you – then write to the Secretary of
State for the Environment asking him to 'call in' the
planning application. Stress the importance of the site
and the strength of local feeling against the development.
Try to get the support of your MP.

If the district council rejects the planning application,
the person who submitted it may appeal to the Secretary
of State for the Environment. The Minister can decide
to overrule the council and grant permission. On the other
hand, he may call a public inquiry at which you will be
able to give evidence to back up your objection. An
additional advantage of an inquiry is that it attracts
media coverage, which may in turn recruit people to your
cause.

Quarries and tips:
Where a site is threatened by quarrying or gravel
extraction, the county council is responsible for dealing
with the planning application. The planning policies are
spelt out in the county minerals plan. If the site is in a
river valley, the regional water authority has to be
consulted about the application.

Waste tipping is a little more complicated because, in
addition to planning permission, it requires licensing
under the Control of Pollution Act. These licences are
issued by county councils in England, and by district

councils in Wales. Before granting a licence, the council has to consult the regional water authority which, in turn, can formally object to the grant of a licence if the tipping would be likely to cause water pollution which would prevent its existing uses. It is worth remembering that waste is *anything* removed from a place where it is no longer needed, and that a licence is needed for the tipping of *all* waste, even waste such as builders' rubble.

Your council's own waste disposal plan will show the location of proposed new refuse tips. If the site you are trying to protect is proposed for refuse tipping, your council has the power to give itself planning permission and grant itself the equivalent of a licence. In such cases, your best chance of saving the site is to write to the Secretary of State asking him to 'call in' the planning application by issuing an Article 4 Direction. This may result in a public inquiry. You should ask him to decide whether or not the site should be licensed for refuse tipping. Again, this may mean a public inquiry.

OUT IN THE COUNTRY

However green our cities may be, it's always good to get out into the countryside. But when you do, always remember that the countryside is under threat just as much as urban open spaces. In the last five years, over 400 SSSIs have been destroyed or damaged. Protecting rural sites can be harder since there are virtually no planning controls on agriculture, and large-scale development schemes can be hard to stop.

However, that's no reason not to be vigilant – there are many examples of small groups of people taking action promptly, and successfully saving pieces of countryside from the bulldozers.

When you're out in the countryside, don't forget that there's another source of problems apart from the farmers – and that's *you!* You can minimize the impact you make quite simply by following the Country Code. Little things like shutting gates may seem unimportant to you, but

to those who make their livelihood from the countryside,
they are crucial.

If you care about SSSIs, it's only logical to care about
all the countryside. There may be plenty of primroses
growing on a roadside verge, but if you and others
following you all dig up just one or two clumps, then all
too soon there will be an empty patch. This may sound
very obvious, but the destruction of the countryside isn't
just about major developments; it's also about the slow
but steady erosion caused by all of us.

BRINGING THE COUNTRYSIDE INTO THE CITY

Nature reserves used to be quiet little woodlands, miles
from anywhere, that were home to some rare orchid or
moth. These days, you may find one much nearer home.
All over Britain, there are more and more urban nature
reserves.

They may be small wooded areas in parks, bits of
unused land between housing estates, or even unused
land inside the old gasworks, but they all provide crucial
habitats for the species that share our towns with us.

Often, all it needs is someone to start the ball rolling.
If you know of a piece of derelict land that's home to birds,
rabbits, or even foxes, why not make it into a safer and
richer habitat? A lot can be achieved with a little
technical advice, a small amount of money and some
physical work.

Small woods can be established, boring grassland can
be turned into a flower-rich meadow, or rubbish-strewn
derelict land into an ecological park. Valuable wildlife
habitats can even be established in private gardens; a
flower-bed can soon be made into a butterfly garden. The
work is fun, especially when groups of people get together,
and the result is a valuable resource which offers lasting
pleasure.

One important rule to remember is that it is best not
to import animals and plants which do not occur naturally

in the area. With exotic alien species, there is always a
risk that they will spread out of control because of the
absence of natural predators. This could have harmful
effects upon other wildlife in the area. To make sure that
you do not end up with this sort of problem, it is worth
seeking advice from the Nature Conservancy Council.

City farms are a recent use of vacant urban land. They
involve setting up community gardens, vegetable plots,
small-scale livestock rearing, bee-keeping and, in a few
cases, fish-farming as well. Many of them include wildlife
areas and educational centres. Their primary function
is to provide a focus for the involvement of the local
community in the creation and management of an
educational and recreational resource. They often provide
useful training in building and other practical skills,
usually in association with schemes funded by the
government's Manpower Services Commission. The
National Federation of City Farms is the most valuable
source of detailed advice.

Small-scale projects, such as local tree-planting, can be carried out by a few people on an informal basis. At the other extreme, tasks such as establishing an ecological park or a city farm, both relatively complex matters, obviously require attention to detail and continuity. This is best achieved by setting up a special organization – a committee or even a charitable trust. A further advantage of a committee or trust is that it has the status needed to attract reputable supporters – some of whom may be willing to serve on the committee or as trustees – and the accountability needed to raise funds for the project.

Finding a suitable site is one of the biggest obstacles to setting up such an ecological park or city farm. Ideally you need a fairly large site, at least an acre and preferably more, which is situated close to a densely populated area from where you can draw support. The difficulty is that vacant land in urban areas is often lined up for development. In such circumstances, it may still be possible to obtain short-term permission to use the site. This may make it worthwhile doing some work to improve its wildlife value, even if it's not worth investing a lot of effort and money in a very ambitious project.

If a planning application is pending, it may be possible, given a sympathetic council, to end up with the granting of permission being conditional upon part of the site being set aside for community use, such as an ecological park or city farm.

RESOURCES

Books:
Angela King and Sue Clifford, *Holding Your Ground: An action guide to local conservation* (Temple Smith, 1985). A practical guide to the protection of wildlife, the landscape and old buildings near where we live.

J. Stephenson, *Planning Procedures* (Northwood Books, 1982). A technical review of the bureaucracy of planning.

W.N. Adams, *Nature's Place: Conservation sites and countryside change* (Allen and Unwin, 1986). Describes the losses of wildlife habitats over the last two hundred years, examines current conservation policies and argues for far-reaching reform to protect the countryside as a whole.

Marion Shoard, *The Theft of the Countryside* (Temple Smith, 1980). A polemical critique of modern farming practice.

Richard Mabey, *The Common Ground: A place for nature in Britain's future?* (Arrow Books, 1980). A powerful and well-written plea for the protection of our vanishing wildlife – the mundane as well as the exotic.

A. Rogers, J. Blunden and N. Curry (editors), *The Countryside Handbook* (Croom Helm, 1985). A very useful source of background information. It reviews relevant legislation and policy documents and also provides thumbnail sketches of the official bodies and non-governmental organizations which are involved in land use issues. Also summarizes some key studies.

Friends of the Earth, *The Countryside Campaigners Manual* (1987). A detailed looseleaf guide for activists. Provides advice upon the tactics and practicalities of how to protect threatened wildlife habitats and traditional landscapes. For further details contact Friends of the Earth.

Organizations:

The British Trust for Conservation Volunteers (36 St Mary's Street, Wallingford, Oxfordshire OX10 0EU). Aims to encourage and facilitate public involvement in practical conservation work in rural and urban areas.

The Council for the Protection of Rural England (4 Hobart Place, London SW1W 0HY). Also Council for the Protection of Rural Wales (Ty Gwyn, 31 High Street, Welshpool, Powys). These bodies are primarily concerned with landscape protection. Very involved in planning issues.

Friends of the Earth (377 City Road, London EC1V 1NA). Activities include campaigns to protect the countryside and wildlife and practical work such as tree planting and creating butterfly gardens.

The Royal Society for Nature Conservation (The Green, Nettleham, Lincoln LN2 2NR). The coordinating organization for the County Naturalists Trusts.

The Ramblers Association (1–5 Wandsworth Road, London SW8 2LJ). Concerned with promoting public access to the countryside.

The Royal Town Planning Institute (26 Portland Place, London W1N 4BE). The professional body for land use planners. Publishes *The Planner*, a useful source of up-to-date information.

Countryside Commission (John Dower House, Crescent Place, Cheltenham, Glos GL50 3RA).

Nature Conservancy Council (Northminster House, Northminster Road, Peterborough, Cambs PE1 1UA).

National Federation of City Farms (The Old Vicarage, 66 Fraser Street, Windmill Hill, Bedminster, Bristol, Avon BS3 4LY). Concerned with the promotion of city farms and community gardens.

11.
ECOLOGICAL ECONOMICS

Economics is not everybody's cup of tea. Indeed, many would agree with those ringing words Edmund Burke uttered more than two hundred years ago: 'The Age of Chivalry is gone. That of sophisters, economists and calculators has succeeded, and the glory of Europe is extinguished forever.'

That may well be the case, but we should no more dismiss economics than we should let people make such a mystery out of it. Mrs Thatcher actually hit the nail on the head when she claimed that looking after the nation's finances was just like housekeeping on a much larger scale. In its original Greek form, that's exactly what economics means: 'managing the house'. The 'house' can refer either to our own country, the management of which appears in bad trouble, or to the whole planet, which seems to be crumbling in pieces around us.

One of the reasons why we are such lousy housekeepers stems from our neglect of a very simple truth: you cannot impose infinite demands on a finite resource. If we go on using up the Earth's non-renewable resources (oil, coal and minerals) at the rate we are now, and at the same time misusing the Earth's renewable resources (fertile soil, clean water and forests) at the rate we are now, then at some stage in the future the whole system is going to fall apart. Those who claim that the fact that it has not done so yet is proof that it never will are dangerous idiots. Technological innovation may well postpone the

final crunch, but it cannot put off the day of reckoning altogether.

As Fritz Schumacher pointed out, what sane businessman would go on using up his *capital* to keep his business afloat if the *interest* from that capital was more than enough to cope with all his needs?

This may all sound very remote from our everyday concerns, from the size of our overdraft, or the price of the proverbial pint of beer. But it isn't. We've already seen in Chapter Three how our power as consumers imposes considerable individual responsibility on us not to abuse that power when it comes to disposing of our income. If we take this idea several stages further, the links between each individual and the state of the planet become even clearer.

SAVER SOVEREIGNTY

With most economic transactions, we do at least have nominal control over what happens to our money. For instance, millions of people in this country put some of their money into shares, or building societies, or pension funds. We hand over to them the responsibility for

129

managing our money in return for whatever dividend or interest we receive. But how many people take the trouble to find out what is actually being done with that money, where it is invested, in what sort of businesses, with what sort of impact on people and the environment?

Occasionally, as with the campaign to persuade people to move their accounts from Barclays Bank because of its extensive business interests in South Africa, one particular target is singled out for attention. Specific pressure groups may even be set up to publicize and campaign against the activities of certain companies, as with the Partizans (People Against Rio Tinto Zinc and Subsidiaries) who act both as a shareholders' pressure group within RTZ and as a research body focusing on the negative impacts resulting from some of RTZ's operations in developing countries.

Campaigns of this sort have served to heighten people's awareness of the need to be informed about the ways in which our money is being used. Of course, it is often very difficult to get that kind of information, which is exactly what brought the Ethical Research and Information Service into being. It can provide details of 'ethical' investment options, and advise on the activities of many companies, to assist would-be investors with a conscience. A similar service is offered by the Stewardship Fund of Friends Provident.

There is clearly a need for new financial institutions that subscribe to this principle of 'saver sovereignty', which would allow people to take a much closer interest in the projects in which they invest. Two of the best examples of such institutions in Britain are the Mercury Provident Society, which tries to fit the concerns and interests of investors with appropriate projects that are seeking funding, and the Ecology Building Society, which only gives loans on properties which promote self-sufficiency and the most ecologically efficient use of land.

Many of these initiatives are still very small, but there

is no doubt that more and more people are beginning to support them. Let us hope it spreads. The notion that savers have a right to sovereignty in the investment of their savings is revolutionary stuff!

PAYING OUR DUES

By contrast, there will inevitably be some economic transactions over which we feel we have no control. When we pay our electricity bills for instance, we can't help but give implicit support to that proportion of our electricity (17%, as it happens) which is provided by nuclear power. But a campaign run by Consumers Against Nuclear Energy (CANE) points out that even in such circumstances, we are *not* powerless. For a start, we can enclose a protest letter with our next electricity bill, even paying that bill with a special 'anti-nuclear cheque' available from CANE. We can also complain directly to our local electricity board, to the Central Electricity Generating Board, to our local Electricity Consultative Council, to our MP, to the Secretary of State for Energy. There's a lot of complaining to be done!

If you want to take it further, CANE organizes a
'withholding campaign' which involves temporarily
withholding a symbolic 17% (to cover the contribution
from nuclear power) of your bill each quarter. The
withheld amount is held in trust by CANE until you
require it, when it is returned to you or paid directly to
the electricity board so that you don't have to get yourself
cut off. Anyone contemplating such action should contact
CANE for all the necessary details before proceeding.

It gets trickier still when we have to consider our role
as taxpayers. Again, when we pay taxes, we hand over
responsibility for the use of that money to a third party
– and have very little choice about it. The chains of
responsibility referred to in Chapter One are obviously
much more extended when it is a question of people acting
on our behalf, through government, rather than us acting
for ourselves. Hardly surprising, once payment is made,
that there is a tendency to let go of the idea that it is
still our money and that we still have a stake, however
small it may be, in how it's spent.

Some people go to considerable lengths to assert that
right. In the same way that some consumers withdraw
17% of their electricity bills to protest against nuclear
power, so some taxpayers refuse to pay that proportion
of their tax bill that is earmarked for military spending
in general or, more specifically, for expenditure on
nuclear weapons. Such a course of action involves
considerable commitment, and people are advised to
contact the Peace Tax Campaign before proceeding.

INTERNATIONAL AID: WHO IS HELPING WHOM?

With other areas of government spending, our stake is
by no means so cut and dried. For instance, a small
proportion of our taxes is used to help people in the
developing world. This aid budget is allocated either
directly, as bilateral aid, or indirectly as multilateral aid,
with the UK making contributions to multilateral
funding agencies such as the World Bank or the European

Development Fund.

A lot of attention has recently been focused on the extent to which these agencies can often do more harm than good. Consider the following projects funded by the World Bank:

- *Indonesia's Transmigration Programme:* The resettling of millions of landless poor from Indonesia's inner islands on the outer islands, which will cause the destruction of an estimated 3.3 million hectares of primary forest within five years. Native West Papuans have already lost 700,000 hectares of their traditional homeland to transmigrants, and 10,000 tribal refugees have fled to seek asylum in Papua New Guinea. World Bank funding for this programme has already exceeded $500 million.

- *India's Narmada Valley Development:* This hydro-power and irrigation scheme will involve the forced relocation of an estimated one million people. The Sardar Sarovar Dam, the first phase of the project, will displace 60,000 tribal people from their traditional lands, mostly with wholly inadequate compensation. Sardar Sarovar is being funded with $300 million from the World Bank.

- *Brazil's Polonoroeste Programme:* This road-building and colonization programme in the Amazon involves the resettling of thousands of peasants in primary rainforest areas. It is estimated that by 1990, an area the size of Britain will have been deforested by the project. The lands of 8,000 Indians have been invaded, causing hundreds of deaths. The Bank's funding of $430 million was suspended after protests in 1985 but has now recommenced, with the social and ecological problems still completely unresolved.

Those are just three disturbing examples of how we, as average taxpayers, contribute to the ecological devastation going on in the Third World. Fortunately, several organizations in this country, including Friends of the Earth, Survival International, Oxfam and the

International Institute for Environment and
Development, are now campaigning for a more
appropriate and responsible use of aid. This pressure has
already proved very effective, both with our own Overseas
Development Administration (the government
department responsible for aid funding) and the World
Bank. Even the biggest and most bureaucratic of agencies
can be obliged to change its ways by the right combination
of campaigning tactics.

INTERNATIONAL DEBT: WHO OWES WHOM?

But the chains of responsibility get even heavier when
you think of our role, as citizens of this particular nation,
in propping up today's desperately unfair international
economic order. To lay it really on the line, how deeply
implicated is each and every one of us in the suffering
and death of millions of people whose governments are
now so in hock to Western banks that for every dollar
they earn through exports, as much as 40% or 50%
disappears in debt repayment? Over the last two years,
public generosity in the face of the African famine has
been overwhelming, producing the greatest volume of
donations ever to the voluntary organizations. The will
of the people in this country is clear – an end to world
hunger. But as Oxfam points out, for every pound we gave
for famine relief in Africa in 1985, Western countries
took back *two* pounds in debt repayment.

When a small country like Peru, overwhelmed by its
burden of debt, starts to lay waste its natural wealth in
order to earn enough to repay both the interest and the
capital owing to the West, how do we allocate
responsibility for the ensuing rape of the Earth and the
further long-term impoverishment of the people? After
all, these are *our* banks and *our* development agencies,
working hand in hand with *our* government, propping
up an economic system of *our* making.

This is not so much a chain of responsibility as of
oppression and enslavement. And yet this was never the

original intention. Foreign aid was meant to have helped poor developing nations gear up their economies to compete successfully in international markets, and to relieve the grinding poverty in which their citizens are trapped. But after three decades of 'concerted international action', over 800 million people still live in absolute poverty, denied the most basic and meagre necessities. During those thirty years, the average increase in per capita income for citizens of the rich nations grew by over $3,900 dollars, while the average increase for the poor grew by a pitiful $50.

The basic cause of this imbalance has been the pursuit of high-growth, export-oriented economies by the governments of developing countries, a strategy designed to bring the benefits of a Western consumer society. But in the scramble for affluence, too many developing governments ignored fundamental issues like agricultural and land reform, the protection of natural resources (often the most obvious or only source of real wealth available), and improving basic water and health facilities.

Prestige, capital-intensive projects, particularly in energy and transport, were favoured instead. As a result, dams, power stations, roads and airports took precedence over providing clean drinking water (4.2 billion people will still need access to clean water and sanitation by 1990, according to the World Health Organization), self-sufficiency in food (every year 40 million people, almost half of them children, die from hunger and hunger-related diseases, according to UNICEF), and the regular supply of wood for cooking and heating (1.5 billion people have difficulty finding such supplies, according to the UN's Food and Agriculture Organization).

On the ground, the effects are there for all to see. Throughout the tropics, examples of inappropriate development abound: dams silting up because watershed catchments have not been protected, failed agricultural projects, long highways which opened up previously inaccessible, fragile ecosystems for development.

Lacking the capital infrastructure of an industrial economy, a manufacturing base or the financial muscle to compete on trading and stock markets, the only way most developing countries can repay the aid loans has been by rapidly increasing cash crop agriculture, or by selling primary raw materials, to earn foreign exchange via exports. The money value of food has become far more important than its nutritional qualities. Far from fighting this tendency, agricultural aid has repeatedly reinforced it, promoting large-scale, single-crop systems with initiatives like the Green Revolution, which rely on heavy inputs of expensive agro-chemicals and machinery.

Under such systems, not only are fewer hungry people fed as the best available land is given over to grow food for export, but it is the already wealthy nations who benefit all round. Having made the loans in the first place, they then receive the food (or other raw materials like minerals or timber) that have to be sold to pay them back. One-fifth of the world's population live in industrial economies, yet they consume 80% of total global resources and enjoy 65% of all income. In the meantime, starving, landless populations throughout the developing world continue to overgraze fragile grasslands, overcut degraded forests, and struggle for water simply to stay alive.

To earn its cash, Ethiopia is cutting the last of its forests to plant coffee; Kenya is felling its forests to grow tea. As drought and famine obliterate the people of the Sahel, bumper harvests of cash crops like cotton and peanuts are recorded from the region. Both Africa and Latin America face severe difficulties feeding their people, yet boast similar surpluses of agricultural commodities. Over 100 countries, lacking self-reliant, sustainable agricultures, depend on grain shipments from the North (which have to be paid for in the midst of increasing poverty and a deteriorating resource base) to survive. In 1984, Africa's cereal import bill was $5.4 billion.

None of this need have happened – and there is

certainly no excuse for it to continue. Even now, although donor agencies are slowly beginning to learn from past mistakes, the 'trickle-down theory' of aid, where the poor are supposed eventually to benefit from grand projects, still pervades development planning. This will only alter when the industrial nations that run aid programmes accept different priorities and encourage sustainable agriculture and forestry to meet the genuine needs of desperate people. When they are hungry or thirsty or cold, people want food, water and fuel – not dams, roads and airports.

Governments change when voters insist they do so. The tragedy of Ethiopia drove home to millions the scale and horror of the problem. In a matter of months, during early 1985, over $400 million of emergency food relief, mostly collected from private sources, flowed into the country. It stopped people starving – for a while. But a crisis response does not solve the long-term problem of preventing the disaster occurring again. That can only be done by restoring the ravaged soil, water and forest resources of Ethiopia, and countries like it.

If we want to cure the problem, we have to accept the

responsibility for what's going on. After all, the aid comes from our money. The least we can do is to make sure that it is used wisely.

WORK AND THE ENVIRONMENT

This kind of international perspective is crucial for any understanding of today's ecological crisis. And the conclusions that we draw from it are equally relevant to our own beleaguered economy. In too many areas, investment is both destructive of the environment and of people's basic right of access to good work. Just consider the following comparison: £14 million this year in Britain will be invested in research into renewable sources of energy, but over £300 million will be invested in nuclear power. This is crazy, not only because those renewables will never become fully viable until we start putting the money up front now, in order to enjoy the dividend later, but also because it works against the need to create new jobs.

It is indeed true that, if nuclear power is phased out over the next ten to fifteen years, as many as 20,000 jobs in the nuclear industry and in supporting industries may be lost. But this is a small number compared to the rapid job losses that have occurred in the coalmining industry, partly as a result of the lower demand for coal caused by the expansion of the nuclear programme. Moreover, increases in employment in other energy industries will more than compensate for the job losses from the nuclear industry.

The money released by phasing out nuclear power could go into projects such as energy conservation or coal-powered combined heat and power schemes, or conventional coal-fired stations. The insulation of ten million of Britain's badly neglected houses, and at least four large inner-city coal-fired CHP schemes, producing as much electricity as 3–4 nuclear power stations, would create employment in inner cities as well as in the engineering industries who would supply components.

It has been calculated that such schemes would create a net additional 250,000 long-term jobs throughout the UK economy over the next fifteen years. Moreover, many of the jobs created would require both limited and extensive training, in stark contrast to the nuclear industry where few jobs are appropriate for today's unemployed youth.

In almost every area of policy, the ecological approach is also the one that is most likely to generate new opportunities for good work. Be it a question of food production, resource management, recycling, land use, pollution control, health policies or transport planning, the answer is the same: we care best for ourselves by caring first for the planet.

This is becoming increasingly apparent not only through the new 'sunrise industries' (bio-technologies, pollution control technologies, recycling and resource substitution technologies, and the environmental services sector) but also at the local level, where amid all the gloom engendered by the tragedy of mass unemployment, many points of light are now beginning to appear. Despite curbs on spending, local authorities have been able to create many permanent jobs in refurbishing the local environment. In 1986, the environmental work already done through the Manpower

Services' Community Programme was given a great boost through the launch of UK2000 under the chairmanship of Richard Branson.

At national, local and community level, a growing concern for the environment has begun to dispel once and for all the old nonsense that economic prosperity and ecological responsibility simply aren't compatible. They may have been a long time coming, but the rapidly emerging alternatives of the Green Movement offer far more hope to far more people than the threadbare promises of yesterday's clapped-out economics.

RESOURCES

Books and periodicals:

By far the most important book on the New Economics is *The Living Economy* edited by Paul Ekins (Routledge and Kegal Paul, 1986), a summary of the deliberations of The Other Economic Summit. It also has a most comprehensive contacts section.

It's still hard to beat Fritz Schumacher's *Small is Beautiful: Economics as if People Mattered* (Abacus, 1974) or his *Good Work* (Sphere, 1979). Another great 'golden oldie' is Hazel Henderson's *Politics of the Solar Age* (Doubleday, New York, 1981).

James Robertson's *The Sane Alternative* (1983) and *Future Work* (Temple Smith/Gower, 1985) provide an excellent overview of the state of alternative ideas about employment. He and Alison Pritchard also produce the newsletter *Turning Point* (The Old Bakehouse, Ilges Lane, Cholsey, Oxford OX10 9NU), which covers a huge range of green interests.

On employment, Charles Handy's *The Future of Work* (Blackwells, 1984) and Guy Dauncey's *The Unemployment Handbook* (National Extension College, Cambridge, 1981) are both very useful. *Fear at Work* by R. Kazis and R. Grossman (Pilgrim Press,

New York, 1982) exposes the myth that environmental protection always costs jobs.

Organizations:

ENVIRONMENT, DEVELOPMENT AND PEACE GROUPS:

Consumers Against Nuclear Energy, PO Box 697, London NW1 8YQ

Friends of the Earth, 377 City Road, London EC1V 1NA

International Institute for Environment and Development, 3 Endsleigh Street, London WC1H 0DD

Oxfam, 274 Banbury Road, Oxford OX2 7DZ

Partizans, 218 Liverpool Road, London N1 1LE

Peace Tax Campaign, 13 Goodwin Street, London N14

Survival International, 29 Craven Street, London WC2N 5NT

GROUPS INVOLVED IN EMPLOYMENT INITIATIVES AND THE NEW ECONOMICS:

British Unemployed Resource Network, 318 Summer Lane, Birmingham B19 3RL

Business Network, 18 Well Walk, London NW3 1LD

Co-operative Development Agency, 20 Albert Embankment, London SE1

Ecology Building Society, 43 Main Street, Cross Hills, via Keighley, West Yorks BD20 8TT

Ethical Investment Research and Information Service, 9 Poland Street, London W1V 3DG

Friends Provident, Pixham End, Dorking, Surrey RH4 1QA

Industrial Common Ownership Movement, 7/8 The Corn Exchange, Leeds LS1 7BP

Mercury Provident, Orlingbury House, Lewes Road, Forest Row, Sussex RH18 5AA

UK2000, 19-21 Rathbone Place, London W1

12.
EDUCATION FOR LIFE

At this stage, no-one should be asking, 'Yes, but what can I do?' As we've seen, there's a vast amount to be done, and more often than not it's up to each one of us to take the initiative to get it done. Not the least of our responsibilities in this respect is to ensure that the next generation makes a rather better job of it than we seem to have done.

A QUESTION OF VALUES

Education begins at home. It really is the primary responsibility of parents to instil in their children the kind of ecologically-oriented values that we will depend on in the future. In matters of diet, health, attitudes to the living world, caring for animals and consumption in general, most young children will take the lead from their parents. There is no more powerful instruction than that provided by a working model; actually doing counts for far more than hours of talk about what we should be doing.

All well and good – in a perfect society! But it's not as easy as that when children are so relentlessly exposed to the values of a competitive, consumption-oriented, throwaway society. It's hard for parents to refuse their child what others seem to take for granted: the endless bags of crisps and bars of chocolate, the apparent delights of takeaway fast-foods, fancy toys, clothes and fashion.

It's particularly difficult to know how to handle the TV, through which that unwritten law of our society that you are what you own, or what you consume, even if you're only six or seven years old, is consistently reinforced. For all the wonderful wildlife documentaries and some excellent educational television, children today are exposed to a regular diet of trivia, violence and distorted, selfish values. At exactly the time when they require the very best, they are being fed the very worst.

THE RIGHT SCHOOLS?

Many parents have unfortunately expressed exactly the same sentiment about the schools which their children attend. They are worried about whether their children are getting the best, or achieving their full potential. From the perspective of the Green Movement, many of the problems stem from the sheer size of today's schools. Schools of around 2,000 pupils were regarded as the optimum size to ensure a full range of subjects and an active sixth form, but as time has gone by, other effects of such size have been felt more immediately. Bureaucracy, ill-discipline, strained relations between teachers and parents, between teachers and children, and between the school and the community – many of these things could be mitigated by smaller schools.

There are several initiatives underway today to try and improve the situation. 'Human scale', as advocated in the writings of Fritz Schumacher and others, is seen as the key feature of this new approach. Perhaps the most succinct version of this appears in the form of a *Manifesto for Education on a Human Scale* (available from Philip Toogood, Chapel Cottage, Fore Street, Hartland, Nr. Bideford, North Devon). The *Manifesto* argues for the following propositions:

- that only in very rare exceptional cases should village primary schools be closed against local and parental wishes
- that large schools wishing to subdivide into federations of smaller units on a single site should be supported
- that existing secondary schools regarded as 'too small' should not normally be closed, and that ways should be explored for them to work co-operatively with other schools and to adopt practices and technologies that compensate for smaller size with supporting advice and services from the local education authority
- that co-operative efforts by parents and others to restore small infant and primary schools to their villages should be considered sympathetically by local education authorities
- that, as in other European countries, small community schools, anxious to work within the state system, should be viewed sympathetically for funding by local education authorities, and their progress and qualities evaluated as examples of good practice.

Many parents are also very concerned about exactly what is taught in schools today. Only recently has the curriculum begun to reflect a growing interest in environmental and development issues, and it is encouraging to see the way in which a large number of schools have incorporated new courses or options in this area. Mainstream subjects like biology and geography, especially under the impetus of the new GCSE exam, have taken on the challenge of making what is taught far more relevant to today's young people.

There are many organizations which are able to give good advice on suitable materials in this area. The Council for Environmental Education is a co-ordinating body promoting environmental education and producing a newssheet listing new resources (which appears ten times a year) and a good magazine. The Conservation Trust also has a comprehensive resource bank which is available on loan to members, and also produces a newsletter and study notes for use by pupils and teachers. Both the British Trust for Conservation Volunteers and the Royal Society for Nature Conservation run excellent schemes to involve young people in voluntary practical conservation work. They also have a schools officer and distribute action packs.

For all that we can seek ways of improving our existing schools, many parents still despair of *any* school coming up with the goods, and now seek a home-based alternative. In 1976, an organization called Education Otherwise was set up by a small group of parents, taking its name from the 1944 Education Act, which states that parents are responsible for their children's education, 'either by regular attendance at school or otherwise'.

It has now evolved as a self-help organization which can offer support, advice and information to families contemplating or practising home-based education as an alternative to schooling. The practice of 'education otherwise' is steadily spreading, and membership has risen to 1,700.

What is really lacking, of course, is some halfway house, something between our monolithic, inflexible state system and complete withdrawal from it. Many people look to the kind of alternative operating in Denmark, where some 10% of children are educated in small, community-based schools. These schools are independent – but still state-funded. Unfortunately, given the stultified thinking about education in all the major parties, such exciting ideas remain a rather distant goal in this country. They are something that all interested parents should be actively campaigning for.

INFORMATION AND PARTICIPATION

There's a lot of truth in the old saying that information is power. Many of the things discussed in this book depend on people being well-informed, and that's not always such an easy matter. The level of secrecy in Britain today has reached proportions that seriously undermine the health of our democracy. In addition to the Official Secrets Act, there are over a hundred statutes making the disclosure of information by civil servants or others a criminal offence, and there is a civil service classification system based on the principle that virtually all documents are either Top Secret, Secret, Confidential or Restricted.

In 1984, the Campaign for Freedom of Information was set up by Des Wilson to bring about the repeal of the Official Secrets Act and to replace it with a Freedom of Information Act, creating a public right of access to official information, and placing upon the information-holders an obligation to disclose. This would not only cover central government, but also local authorities and all statutory bodies. It would also place upon organizations in the private sector an obligation to give access to and disclose such information as may be required by the public interest.

The struggle for freedom of information is just one aspect of all that has to be done to defend our democratic rights and privileges. We live in difficult times: the control of the mass media, an increase in centralized data banks, impersonal surveillance and 'precautionary' telephone-tapping, the suspension of certain trade union rights, a widening of wealth differentials, a 'survival of the fittest' philosophy, the steady military build-up, an increase in political terrorism, and above all the erosion of local democracy – these are the hallmarks of a society

that has become complacent about its basic rights.

All of these things threaten the vitality of our democracy – and all those who see themselves as green depend on the maintenance of that democracy, however many reservations we may have about its fairness or effectiveness. The only antidote to alienation, indifference and apathy (which provide the seedbed for those whose politics make them contemptuous of democracy) is participation, getting stuck in, getting involved wherever and whenever possible.

The trouble is that, once people have cast their vote, they are often tempted to consider that the end of it. To a certain extent, such an attitude is understandable; there really isn't much you can do until the next election comes round! But the real trouble is that most people end up being represented by someone they didn't vote for, either because they voted for someone else, or because they didn't vote at all. This is one of the worst consequences of the ridiculous British first-past-the-post system.

Part of the answer to this is to change the system, adopting some form of proportional representation as in most other European countries. With the single transferrable vote system, constituencies would be much larger, returning five or six MPs of different parties, rather than just one as at present. Proportional representation would also have a considerable impact on local politics, and perhaps reduce some of the mind-numbing allegiance to party labels which currently serves as a great disincentive to people wanting to get involved at the local level.

Many of the changes we have been pressing for in this book can only be brought about by radical measures of decentralization, bringing decision-making down to the level at which people are directly affected.

And, at the end of the day, however much we manage to participate in the political process, we have to come right back down again to what each individual can do. You may already be eating more fibre and less meat; you may be taking greater care of your health; you may be recycling your *Guardian* and filling up your bottle bank; you may have insulated your home; you may be much more conscious of your responsibilities as a consumer; you may be using lead-free petrol, or even have given up your car in favour of a bicycle; you may therefore be feeling that's enough!

But it's not. You've just reached first base. There's now a long climb ahead, and for this you will need others to be climbing with you, if only to lighten those chains of responsibility. Going green isn't easy. It's possibly the greatest personal challenge you will ever take on – but what's the alternative?

RESOURCES

Books:
John Holt, *Teach your Own*
  (Lighthouse Books, 1982)
Ivan Illich, *Deschooling Society*
  (Marion Boyars, 1970)
Carl Rogers, *Freedom to Learn in the Eighties*
  (1983)

Philip Toogood,
  The Head's Tale (1984)

Magazines:

Green Teacher, a new bi-monthly magazine, can be
  contacted at Llys Awel, 22 Heol, Pentrerhegyn,
  Machynlleth, Powys, Wales.

Resurgence also carries good articles on education (see
  Resources Section for Chapter Two, page 27).

Organizations:

Council for Environmental Education, School of
  Education, University of Reading, London Rd,
  Reading, Berks RG1 5AQ

Conservation Trust, George Palmer School,
  Northumberland Ave, Reading, Berks RG2 0EN

Education Otherwise, 25 Common Lane, Hemmingford
  Abbots, Cambridge PE1 9AN

British Trust for Conservation Volunteers, 36 St Mary's
  St, Wallingford, Oxon OX10 0EU

Royal Society for Nature Conservation, The Green,
  Nettleham, Lincoln LN2 2NR

APPENDIX: CAMPAIGNING

If you want something done – *do it yourself!*

Things stay the same because some people like it that way. If you're going to change anything, you've got to make certain people take certain decisions, sometimes about things that they have never thought about before. The single biggest obstacle to change is the idea that 'it's always been like that so it has to carry on being like that'.

You can change some aspects of your environment yourself – that's what this book has been about. But often you'll realize you can't do it all on your own. Be it stopping a nuclear power station being built or getting a zebra crossing down your street, there are times when you need friends and allies. What you'll also need is a plan of action. And you may be surprised to find that it often doesn't matter what the problem is – you go about solving it in exactly the same way.

This appendix offers some brief guidelines on how to get a campaign going on any issue in your locality. This is not a set of rules because there are none, but the ways to a successful conclusion are usually very similar. Des Wilson, former Chairman of Friends of the Earth, has written two books on the subject, both of which should be essential reading for anyone about to launch a campaign, and which expand greatly on the guidelines that follow.

GETTING STARTED

You'll only realize that a campaign is needed when a crisis hits – Friends of the Earth often gets rung up by people who've just noticed that bulldozers are destroying their favourite piece of woodland. So lesson one is: keep your eyes open. Changes to your local environment will usually need planning permission. Planning permission is granted by your local council and they will have a duty to publish all applications that are made to them. These will usually appear weekly in your local paper, and if you do care about your local environment, one of the most important things you can do is to spend three minutes a week checking through the week's list in the paper. Most of them will be totally innocuous, but if there's going to be any major disturbance, it will surface here early on.

Let's assume you've seen that application to turn that piece of 'derelict land' that is in fact your favourite piece of local woodland into an industrial estate. Lesson two is: object early and object loud. Send in your letter of objection to the Planning Officer of the local authority, send copies to your local councillors, and also to your local papers with a covering letter explaining why it's important. Don't worry about it for days or weeks; don't wait to talk to other people; if you're worried, *object*! You can always withdraw an objection, but if you miss the deadline you may lose the issue there and then. Don't ever say: 'Oh I expect plenty of other people are objecting.'

Now take the time to think. Don't rush to get a campaign going immediately. The problem you are facing may seem very real and serious, but don't plunge in without knowing exactly what you are doing.

PLANNING YOUR CAMPAIGN

The purpose of any campaign is to win. The first question, therefore, is: what do you want to win? Pin down your campaign aim to one sentence so that you can tell the press, not that 'we are campaigning to preserve the natural beauty of our unique and threatened environment', but that 'we are campaigning to prevent the destruction of Hundred Acre Wood by MegaBuck Developers Ltd'. That statement tells people what you are worried about and the name of your 'opponent'.

The other important word in that sentence is 'we'. You can't do it on your own. The first support should come from friends and acquaintances. If you can't convince some of them, you'll never succeed (but don't bore all your friends to death). Sit down with them, think about the issue, and ask yourself one crucial question: can we win? It may seem unlikely that you will, but almost always there is some way you will see to influence events in your direction. If there isn't, don't waste your time. Confine yourself to a protest letter and go and do something else. We can't win them all!

But you'll probably find some way forward. In the case of a local development, this may hinge on the local council. Your aim is now to stop the destruction of Hundred Acre Wood by persuading the council to refuse MegaBuck Developers planning permission. That gives you the 'target', in this case the council.

So find out about your council. Do you know any councillors? Do you know anyone who does? Your local library will have the names and addresses of them all along with the names of those crucial councillors on the Planning Sub-Committee. Now put yourself in the position of the councillors. Why should they accept or refuse this development? It may be that they will favour it because your town needs a new industrial estate to create jobs. So clearly you must make sure that your campaign is not seen as being against industrial development, but against it in this area.

This brings us on to the next crucial question: what is the alternative? Whatever the campaign, you need to have an alternative. If it's a land use issue, the answer may be in the structure plan. This is a document put together by the local council in consultation with local people and organizations. It will recommend that some areas be scheduled for housing, some for industry, some for open spaces and so on. If the land in question is not zoned for development you are in a very strong position, and it is quite likely the council will throw out the application. But don't bank on it!

BUILDING SUPPORT

You need as much support as you can get. So think: who uses the wood? who's going to be affected? who'll support you? Local residents – your neighbours even – are a good start. Has the area any importance as a nature site? Contact your local Naturalists Trust who will be able to tell you and who may well support you. Is it of historical importance? In this case the Civic Society may be a valuable ally.

Cast your net as wide as you can about whom to approach – at worst they can only say no. But don't approach any of them until you're ready – the launch of your campaign should be carefully planned.

LAUNCHING THE CAMPAIGN

This is crucial – the point at which you go out to get public support. For the campaign launch it is a good idea to have several things ready:

- a leaflet describing your concerns; it should say where the site is, what you see as an alternative, what damage the proposed development would do, etc.
- a petition form; petitions can be effective if a large number of local people sign them. They're also good for making people think about the issue
- a press release. This should be a short notice to the press, explaining why you're doing what you're doing. It should be typed (double-spaced), short and concise, with a headline that explains the campaign

153

(e.g. '"Save our Wood" say local residents'), with a phone number and address of whoever will handle the press. This should be delivered to the press in advance of your launch date and followed up with a phone call to a reporter. You can 'embargo' press releases. This means sending them out a few days in advance with a note on them saying 'Not to be used until . . .' The press will honour these since it is in their interests to do so

- a poster with a good slogan is always useful, both to publicize the campaign and to act as a visual backdrop for any photos. A clever designer is a valuable ally for any campaign!

- badges and stickers are also useful, both to get the message across and to raise some money (though do not expect to make a lot – making them can be an expensive business).

Equipped with all this you should be ready to go. Launch the campaign with something visual to attract the local press photographers – half a dozen people with banners in the wood is far better than a staid press conference (which the press probably won't attend anyway, since your press work in advance will – or should – have told them all they need to know). In town, organize a leafleting session or set up a stall with petitions in the marketplace, and make sure the press know whom to contact to give them all the details.

THE MEETING

One of the mainstays of local campaigning is the public meeting. This can be a chance for concerned people to meet each other, to discuss the issue, to hear why their concerns are justified, and to come away feeling inspired. Unfortunately a badly organized meeting can leave people feeling alienated or bored.

So, do it properly! Make sure it is well publicized with posters, leaflets, and mentions in the local press and on radio, find good speakers, and invite local 'dignitaries' (councillors, MPs, local names). This will be a chance for you to involve a large number of new people in your campaign, so use it well.

There are a great many 'dos' and 'don'ts' about meetings, and these are well described in the recommended books, but above all remember to get the names and addresses of everyone who attends. The very fact that they did attend means they're interested.

AND ON WITH THE CAMPAIGN!

By now you should be involved in a developing campaign group. The important thing is to make sure the campaign develops as well! A large number of members does not necessarily make a campaign more successful than a very few. Make sure that everyone involved is writing letters to the council, to councillors, to MPs, to the press. It may sound mundane, but it does produce results.

After the initial phase, the council will probably be considering the issue in committee. You should by now have found out who's on the relevant committee, so write to them or ring them and ask to meet beforehand. Lobbying councillors is something the developers will certainly be doing, so you should too. Discuss the issue reasonably and slowly, showing them why you're worried, and where appropriate what your alternative plans are. Remember: very few councillors ever get elected because they are concerned about the environment, so don't expect them to be fully informed. It's your job to make them that way.

The council committee may throw out the proposal or pass it on to the full council. You can defeat it there, or get it referred back to the committee. All this can take several months, especially if they are getting consistent and well-researched objections. So keep up the pressure!

There are endless examples of where small groups have won great victories just because they took the trouble.

Inevitably this outline is sketchy and can only point

you in the right direction. As you build your campaign you'll find unexpected allies in many places. Don't be afraid to come to Friends of the Earth or any other pressure group for assistance. Every environmental disaster starts in someone's backyard; and that's also the best place to start fighting it.

RESOURCES

Books:
The best two books on local campaigning in Britain are both by Des Wilson. They are:
Pressure: The A-Z of Campaigning in Britain (Heinemann, 1984)
Citizen Action: Taking Action in Your Community (Longman, 1986)
Holding Your Ground by Angela King and Sue Clifford (Temple Smith, 1985) is a book by the Common Ground organization, and is a detailed look at how you can protect the things you care about in your locality.

Organizations:
Friends of the Earth have 220 local groups around the country who may be able to help you. Contact FoE for more details.
The Town and Country Planning Association has a great deal of material on how the planning system works, and the Planning Aid Service can be invaluable. Contact them at 17 Carlton House Terrace, London SW1.
The Council for the Protection of Rural England is actively campaigning to protect what is left of our countryside. Their address is 4 Hobart Place, London SW1.

ABOUT FRIENDS OF THE EARTH

Friends of the Earth is a national campaigning organization, established in Britain in 1971, with a network of 220 local groups and 26,000 national supporters. Each group is financially independent and decides its own policies and priorities. In practice, groups support national campaigns, and also initiate campaigns on local issues.

In addition there are Friends of the Earth groups in 28 countries in four continents, all linked under the umbrella of Friends of the Earth International. A small secretariat is based in the Netherlands.

Friends of the Earth first hit the headlines in 1971 when it dumped 1,500 throwaway bottles on the doorstep of Schweppes, the soft drinks manufacturer. Since then, always backed by excellent research, we have used a variety of imaginative methods to get the environmental message across and to influence decision-makers. Thousands of people have participated in consumer pressure campaigns, protests against acid rain, direct action to stop the destruction of irreplaceable wildlife sites, public meetings to stop nuclear waste dumps, cycle rallies, and many more. In addition, Friends of the Earth has published reports, promoted legislation in Parliament and participated in public inquiries.

Friends of the Earth is politically impartial and works with all political parties and other organizations wherever there are areas of agreement.

If you are interested in joining Friends of the Earth, contact the London office (377 City Road, London EC1V 1NA; tel. 01-837 0731) for information about membership and details of groups in your area.

INDEX